"Michael Stelzner IS white papers. And this excellent how-to guide not only tells you everything you need to know to penetrate this lucrative writing niche AND produce a top-quality product, but does it with a fun, engaging voice."

Peter Bowerman, Author, The Well-Fed Writer *series, and* The Well-Fed Self-Publisher, *WellFedWriter.com*

"What a fantastic resource! This is the definitive guide to intelligent lead generation using white papers."

Andrew Goodman, Author, Winning Results with Google AdWords

"Michael Stelzner is widely recognized as a top white paper writer and a guru in marketing with white papers. By reading his excellent book on the subject, you can master in a few evenings the white paper marketing principles it has taken Michael years to develop and perfect."

Robert W. Bly, Author, The White Paper Marketing Handbook *(Thomson)*

"This book will pay for itself faster than almost any other investment I can imagine. No doubt all of your writing, not just your white papers, will improve as a result. Michael's riff about being generic is a must-read."

Seth Godin, Author, Small Is the New Big

"Michael Stelzner is the 'King of White Papers.' This is a book I recommend to all of my readers and clients!"

Lori Richardson, Sales Coach, Trainer, and Author, ScoreMoreSales.com

"As a freelance copywriter, this book is worth its weight in gold. In my opinion, it is the definitive guide to the best practices of white paper research, planning, writing and editing. I'm not sure how I ever did without it."

Steve Slaunwhite, Copywriting Expert and Author of Secrets of Six-Figure Freelancing

"Michael Stelzner's *Writing White Papers* is a terrific guide for everyone, including the pro who writes and markets with white papers. The chapter on creating a compelling title by itself is worth the price of the book!"

David Meerman Scott, Author, Cashing In With Content: How Innovative Marketers Use Digital Information to Turn Browsers Into Buyers

"Because it is packed full with practical, step-by-step instructions, this book is a valuable tool for every marketer. *Writing White Papers* should definitely be an ongoing resource for marketers and a must-have for their bookshelves!"

Heather Foster, Director of Marketing, KnowledgeStorm

"Dump those worthless brochures right now! Instead, arm your sales force with well-written white papers. Learn how to do them right with *Writing White Papers*!"

Jill Konrath, Author, Selling to Big Companies *and Chief Sales Officer, SellingtoBigCompanies.com*

"Stelzner's *Writing White Papers* provides marketers with a clear blueprint for creating and marketing successful white papers. This book is a fantastic addition to any business marketer's reading list."

Peter Spande, Director, TechRepublic.com and ITPapers.com

"Is it a good book? It's an excellent book. Whether you are employed or a freelancer, Stelzner's book tells you everything you need to know about writing white papers. Better still, it shows you how to write really, really good white papers."

Nick Usborne, Author, Net Words: Creating High-Impact Online Copy, *FreelanceWritingSuccess.com*

"Both experienced professionals as well as business and technical students will benefit from Mike's pragmatic and direct style that guides the reader through the history and use of white papers, down to the nuts and bolts of putting one together and molding it to the intended audience."

Jim Happel, System Engineering Faculty, Whiting School of Engineering, The Johns Hopkins University

"Michael Stelzner's new book provides a road map that every white paper producer should follow."

Barry Harrigan, Founder, Ziff Davis Web Buyer's Guide & White Paper Library

"Michael Stelzner's book gives readers a double dose of helpful information: research to show how important white papers can be, and advice based on his extensive experience. Students will benefit from Stelzner's step-by-step approach."

Russell Willerton, Ph.D., Technical Communication Program, Boise State University

"Stelzner's book offers a compelling case for the essential place of white papers in thought leadership, decision-making and policy-setting. *Writing White Papers* can serve both as a sourcebook for writers in marketing, industry and government and as a textbook that adds to the repertoire of instructors and students of writing. A necessary and timely book."

James H. Collier, Assistant Professor, Department of English, Virginia Tech

"This book is sure to become the standard reference in its field."

Gordon Graham, Copywriting Expert, ThatWhitePaperGuy.com

Michael A. Stelzner

WRITING
WHITE
PAPERS

HOW TO CAPTURE READERS AND KEEP THEM ENGAGED

WhitePaperSource Publishing
Poway, California
2007

Visit our website, www.whitepapersource.com.

First Edition

ISBN-13: 978-0-9777169-3-7
ISBN-10: 0-9777169-3-7

Library of Congress Control Number: 2006924256

Printed in the United States of America. This book printed on acid-free paper.

The author is grateful for permission to use the following previously copyrighted material: Versera Performance Learning white paper, One Touch Global Technologies white paper and ConnectDirect syndication questions.

Publisher's Cataloging-in-Publication data
Stelzner, Michael Allen.
   Writing white papers : how to capture readers and keep them engaged / Michael A. Stelzner.
   p. cm.
   Includes bibliographical references and index.
   ISBN 0-9777169-3-7

1. Technical writing--Handbooks, manuals, etc. 2. Communication of technical information--Handbooks, manuals, etc. 3. Business writing-- Handbooks, manuals, etc.. 4. High technology--marketing. I. Title.

T11 .S71 W75 2007
808.0666--dc22   2006924256

ATTN: QUANTITY DISCOUNTS ARE AVAILABLE TO YOUR COMPANY, EDUCATIONAL INSTITUTION OR PROFESSIONAL ORGANIZATION for reselling, educational purposes, subscription incentives, gifts or fundraising campaigns.

For more information, please contact the publisher at
WhitePaperSource Publishing,
13025 Danielson Street, Suite 108, Poway, CA 92064
858-748-7800—orders@whitepapersource.com

ACKNOWLEDGMENTS

I want to thank my many clients and colleagues who have helped me refine the ideas and concepts in this book over the last 10 years. The countless hours we have spent together have taught me much.

A special thank you to the WhitePaperSource Forum members who provided a great sounding board for many concepts in this book. I want to especially thank Nettie Hartsock for lighting a fire under me and encouraging me to finish this book. Thanks go out to my editor Lisa Hernandez and my cover designer Michael Warrell.

Lastly, I want to thank my family for supporting me through the laborious process of creating this book.

CONTENTS

INTRODUCTION

In the far off distance, you hear a muffled, repeating sound—ring, ring... Reaching for the phone, you wonder who could be calling at this hour. "Hello?" A voice you recognize—your boss or a client—frantically shouts, "We need to produce a white paper for the trade show and you need to get started—RIGHT NOW!" Your heart races, your eyes widen and you wonder if this is a nightmare. Crawling out of bed, you grab pen and paper, and stare blankly at the wall.

For many of us, this scenario is reality. The task of writing a white paper can be intimidating and is by no means easy. Consider that more than 70 percent of writers rated writing their first white paper as a challenging task.[1] However, there is hope.

This book is your personal Sherpa. It will guide you through unfamiliar terrain and toward the top of the mountain, where your powerful and compelling paper awaits you.

You will learn about every topic related to writing white papers, from establishing a needs assessment to developing compelling content to collecting sales leads with your finished masterpiece.

Breathe deep and do not despair, everything you need is contained within these pages.

My Story: From Observations to White Papers

It all began when I was really young and infatuated with taking things apart and putting them back together. The first thing I remember disassembling was an old record player—much older than I was. Over the years I began observing things and writing about them. I recall rides on the bus and the interesting behaviors of the "regu-

---

[1] Stelzner, M. (November 2005). *WhitePaperSource*. 2005 White paper writer industry survey: Identifying trends and issues faced by white paper writers, http://www.whitepapersource.com/report/.

lars." By the time I exited graduate school I had written hundreds of unpublished observations on life. Later, writing white papers would become my life.

My first computer was a Commodore VIC-20, which I quickly upgraded to a Commodore 64. As a young college student, I was the first among my friends to have a computer and printer. I used my "machine" to create compelling reports and document my strange thoughts. When I entered graduate school, I began conducting research and submitting my findings to trade journals. This was the closest I came to creating something that paralleled a white paper.

While in graduate school, I worked for a rather large value-added reseller as a marketing analyst. That job involved taking a hard look at computer products and producing marketing tools to help the sales force sell. The concept of a white paper was first introduced to me while I was managing a high-performance storage product line. The paper was written by some Berkeley folks known as Patterson, Gibson and Katz, and was titled *A Case for Redundant Arrays of Inexpensive Disks (RAID)*—a rather scientific paper.[2]

Later, I decided to go independent. In the mid-1990s, while working as a product launch specialist for a client, I was tasked with writing my first white paper, a frankly foreign process to me at the time. That paper was poorly titled, *The Value of ATL's High-Availability Libraries.*

Prior to writing that white paper, I had helped the company launch many of its products by creating a series of marketing documents. To create these collateral suites, I had to go back into the labs and sit with engineers to fully understand the inner workings of their refrigerator-sized robotic products. Converting their technical jargon into something that would make sense to the information technology (IT) person buying the product was a challenge. Going through that translation process helped set

---

[2] See http://www-2.cs.cmu.edu/~garth/RAIDpaper/Patterson88.pdf.

the stage for much of the writing philosophy I discuss in this book.

As I began to focus my efforts on producing white papers, I started seeing recurring problems when I engaged new clients. My customers did not fully under-stand how to properly approach a white paper. In addition, most companies wanted to talk exclusively about their products and services. Those self-focused writing approaches contained too many overt marketing messages, a turnoff to most readers.

In 2003, I wrote a paper titled, *How to Write a White Paper: A White Paper on White Papers*. In that paper, I explained the importance of focusing on the needs of readers rather than on one's own selfish desires.[3] Major universities such as Massachusetts Institute of Technology and John Hopkins used the paper in their graduate programs. By the end of 2005, more than 27,000 people had requested a copy. The large numbers of writers seeking to understand how to produce white papers surprised me.

In early 2004, I saw a need for an industry newsletter dedicated to the topics of writing and marketing white papers, and launched the *WhitePaperSource™ News-letter*.[4] My goal was to bring the world's best writers and marketing professionals together to discuss white paper techniques and strategies, and ultimately to further the acceptance of white papers as potent marketing tools.

Later in 2004, I launched WhitePaperSource.com, a white paper portal that includes an active discussion forum on white paper topics and many original articles on writing and marketing white papers. With the news-letter's more than 20,000 subscribers and the site's wide following, I was able to capture insights that would have been otherwise impossible.

Over the years, I proceeded to write nearly 100 white papers on topics ranging from artificial intelligence to

---

[3] See http://www.stelzner.com/copy-HowTo-whitepapers.php.
[4] Subscribe for free at http://www.whitepapersource.com/newsletter/.

retirement housing for companies such as Microsoft, Motorola, HP, SAP, FedEx, Cardinal Health, Monster and many others. I have also presented at national conventions, major universities and large corporations on the topic of writing white papers.

All of this naturally led to the foundation for this book. It is my sincere hope that you gain some powerful insights into how to develop effective white papers.

About This Book

Walk into any major bookstore and you might see hundreds of books on writing, ranging from language use to self-publishing. In your search for books on the topic of white papers, you will notice a total absence of resources on the subject, as there is no book dedicated to the art of writing white papers. This book aims to fill the void. In it, you will learn practical processes and the core elements of creating compelling white papers. Fluff-free, this book is meant to be a comprehensive guide that enables you to create something that will work well.

If you are new to white papers, I suggest you begin with Chapter 1 for a comprehensive overview and read the book straight through. However, if you are familiar with white papers or want to fast-track your white paper writing, start at Chapter 3 to establish an outline, then move over to Chapter 6 for help on the first page and on to Chapter 8 to develop the core of your white paper. Be sure to refer to the appendixes for samples and additional guidance.

I also encourage you to visit WritingWhitePapers.com, a companion website for this book.

✳ Chapter 1 ✳

A Primer on White Papers

White papers help people make decisions. They sit at the forefront of an educational marketing revolution. Powerful enough to lure readers and able to persuade with unyielding strength, the well-written white paper is a super weapon in the marketing professional's arsenal.

Wearing many hats, the white paper can talk business or converse technically, and it can inform or influence. Best of all—it is highly sought after.

The white paper's underlying strength rests on this premise: **If you give readers something of value, they will give you their loyalty, and ultimately their business.**

White papers present monumental opportunities for writers, marketing professionals and businesses. Crafting the white paper can be a rewarding and often profitable experience. A single well-written white paper can propel a business to the thought leadership position and lead to enormous business opportunities. When you author a successful white paper, its positive results are credited to your efforts.

The use of white papers is exploding. In 2001, a Google™ search on the phrase *white papers* returned a

mere 1 million responses.[1] By 2006, that number was
a whopping 329 million! Along with the upward trend,
the term *white paper* has become a fuzzy label, wrongly
applied to many documents. The goal of this chapter is to
clearly define *white paper*, explain why white papers are
important and examine how they are used.

WHAT IS A WHITE PAPER?

Defining a white paper is one of those challenges people
have been wrestling with for some time. If you look up the
term in a dictionary, you will find an outdated response
describing a government report. Let's shed a little light on
the term *white paper* by considering what some respected
experts have to say.

Gordon Graham, an experienced white paper writer,
describes white papers as persuasive essays and observes
that their style rests "somewhere between a lively magazine article and a dry-as-dust academic paper." He adds
that white papers are fact-driven and contain useful
information, expert opinions and ironclad logic.

White papers are tools used to create a positive image
of a company in the eyes of its readership, explains Dr.
Russell Willerton, a professor from Boise State University
who specializes in white papers.

According to veteran white paper writer Jonathan
Kantor, white papers reveal product or service features
and translate them into business advantages.

Extending these thoughts, here are a few concise definitions:

High-level white paper definition: A white paper is a
persuasive document that usually describes problems and
how to solve them. The white paper is a crossbreed of a
magazine article and a brochure. It takes the objective and
educational approach of an article and weaves in persuasive corporate messages typically found in brochures.

---

[1] Graham, G. (2001). The art of the white paper, http://
www.gordonandgordon.com/STC_Chicago.html.

Detailed white paper definition: A white paper is a technical or business benefits document that introduces a challenge faced by its readers and makes a strong case why a particular approach to solving the problem is preferred. A white paper usually proposes a solution to a problem, but can also introduce a new concept or describe how to perform technical tasks. Most white papers range from 6 to 12 pages in length; however, some can exceed 50 pages. White papers are comprised of mostly text and usually very few graphics. However, diagrams, charts and illustrations are commonly included in most white papers.

White papers "represent an intersection of technical documentation (i.e., providing technical information about a product or service) with marketing communication (developing information to inform potential customers, improve sales and garner attention in the marketplace)," explains Willerton.[2]

White Paper History

The term *white paper* is an offshoot of the term *white book*, which is an official publication of a national government. A famous historic white paper is the *British White Paper of 1922* (also known as the *Churchill White Paper*), which addressed political conflict in Palestine.[3] Although white papers have their roots in governmental policy, they have become a common tool used to introduce technology innovations and products. A typical search on the phrase *white paper* will return millions of results, with many focused on technology-related issues.

---

[2] Willerton, D. R. (May 2005). Ethos and exigence: White papers in high-tech industries [Dissertation].
[3] See http://www.palestinefacts.org/pf_mandate_whitepaper_1922.php.

White papers usually provide valuable information to their intended audience, yet readers of white papers generally understand that the sponsoring company is marketing to them. The marketing aspect of a white paper is typically a very soft sell. Overt marketing messages are usually left for other documents. Often, solutions are introduced only after a significant case has been established, demonstrating a clear need.

There are four primary types of white papers:

White Paper Type	Definition
Technical	Technical white papers tend to be targeted at engineers. They often describe processes and procedures with precise detail. These types of white papers are usually introduced during the sales process to describe how things work. In the past, technical white papers were the most common type of white paper. However, most modern white papers are typically focused on business-related topics.
Business Benefits	Business benefits white papers are usually targeted at decision-makers in management positions. These types of white papers often describe the business advantages of implementing solutions and are typically used to generate leads. In recent years, the business application of white papers has grown significantly.
Hybrid Technical/ Business Benefits	Hybrid white papers are usually targeted at both influencers and decision makers. They usually lead with business benefits and include technical descriptions of processes. Hybrid papers are often used as lead generation documents and during the sales process.
Government	Government white papers usually discuss the implication of policy decisions. They are frequently focused at a very narrow audience.

WHY WHITE PAPERS MATTER

White papers help people make decisions. Those decisions range from closing a deal to picking up the phone and initiating contact. White papers are also commonly used to help justify a purchase decision.

The decision to produce a white paper usually stems from the need to sell products and services. Interestingly, the same can be said of brochures, PowerPoint presentations and case studies. What differentiates white papers is their attractiveness to specific types of audiences, including engineers, business executives and other key decision-makers.

Often a white paper will work its way across the desks of an organization in a way that no other document could ever hope to achieve. White papers are able to fly under the radar and penetrate most organizations' anti-marketing defenses because they are sought after and brought into the organization by decision-makers. If they are well-written, white papers will not only reach their target, they will influence them.

White papers can be very persuasive marketing tools. When a good white paper lands in front of the right person, it is a highly effective lead generation and sales instrument. Research indicates that IT executives examine an average of 30 white papers each year, that nearly 90 percent of executives find white papers helpful or extremely helpful and more than half claim white papers influence their buying decisions.[4]

The overwhelming majority of technology marketing professionals—85 percent—acknowledge that white papers are important tools for generating leads.[5] Nearly two-thirds of IT marketers rate white papers as one of the

---

[4] Bitpipe. (February 2004). Bitpipe network user study: Readership usage of white papers in the IT buying process, http://www.bitpipe.com.
[5] TechTarget, Bitpipe and Sam Whitmore Media Survey. (December 2004). 2005 IT marketing trends study results, http://www.techtarget.com.

most effective forms of lead generation.[6] For example, IT professionals respond to an online advertisement's white paper offering more than anything else.[7]

Among the significant breadth of content available to IT professionals, vendor white papers are more frequently read than reviews, analyst reports, product literature, websites, articles or case studies.[8] Furthermore, 86 percent of IT marketers indicate that white papers are effective for generating leads and rank them as more valuable than webinars, free trials, seminars and newsletters.[9]

The gestation period from receipt of a white paper to sale can range from the same day to many months. When asking clients how they found out about my business, the response has often been, "I registered for your white paper a few months back." In some cases, it was more than a year between when a client registered for a white paper and called to inquire about our services. Thus, white papers can have a very long shelf life and if well-written can become viral marketing documents.

In addition, white papers provide a great opportunity to introduce a new concept or show industry thought leadership. Often, professional organizations will highlight a good white paper and suggest it to their members.

WHY YOU SHOULD CARE ABOUT WHITE PAPERS

Writing an effective and persuasive white paper for your company or client can be extremely rewarding. Often,

---

[6] MarketingSherpa. (2004). IT marketing metrics guide: 2004 data for software, hardware & services marketers, http://www.e-consultancy.com/knowledge/whitepapers/90014/it-marketing-metrics-guide-2004-data-for-software-hardware-amp-services-marketers-executive-summary.html.
[7] MarketingSherpa and CMP Media. (2005). 2005 Attitudes and online IT advertising survey, http://www.marketingsherpa.com.
[8] CMO Council and KnowledgeStorm. (September 2005). Define what's valued online, http://www.knowledgestorm.com.
[9] MarketingSherpa. (2005). IT marketing benchmark guide 2005-2006, http://www.marketingsherpa.com.

the document becomes a foundational piece that can be leveraged for many other projects, including presentations, contributed articles and website content.

Because of the amazing marketing ability of a well-written white paper, your efforts can result in significant praise and long-term gain for the business. In addition, the educational value of a white paper can be used not only to inform potential customers, but also may be leveraged to train new employees.

For freelance writers, white papers represent one of the most profitable forms of writing. Word for word, there is no other type of writing that pays as well as white papers. Some of the most experienced white paper writers charge up to $1000 per page.[10]

White papers can also bring significant recognition to the writer. Many writers place their names on the byline of a white paper. If the white paper is well-received in your industry or goes viral, your name will be associated with the excellent ideas presented in your paper.

Why Do Businesses Produce White Papers?

Graham notes that businesses use white papers "to move prospects into the sales funnel and coax them down through it." He notes that this is possible because white papers provide useful information, answer repetitive questions better than a salesperson and help a company gain credibility. Kantor backs this up by adding that "business decision-makers look to white papers to aid them in the decision-making process."

Willerton takes a stronger position and claims that businesses need white papers to "survive in their respective markets." He explains that white papers are written to establish trust in the eyes of potential customers.

White papers also provide businesses the opportunity to take the thought leadership position in an industry by

---

[10] To learn what the current rates are for white paper writers, see http://www.whitepapersource.com/report/.

educating the masses. Thought leadership is the process of establishing a leading idea that is ultimately embraced by an industry. Establishing thought leadership is an underlying goal of many white papers.

HOW WHITE PAPERS ARE USED

White papers are generally produced for one of three reasons: to generate leads, to demonstrate thought leadership or to help close sales.

Purpose	Explanation
Lead Generation	Most organizations will leverage their corporate website, online advertising campaigns or white paper syndication networks to generate leads with white papers. Additionally, many direct mail and traditional advertisements use the white paper as a call to action.
Thought Leadership	Often, businesses will write white papers on concepts that are theoretical or discuss the future of an industry or technology. Thought leadership papers are typically written to demonstrate forward thinking, to help convince existing customers to stick with a company and to persuade the world to buy in to a future vision. These types of white papers convert nicely into trade publication articles.
Close Sales	White papers are often used in the later stages of a sales cycle; as a "leave behind" after a client meeting. While white papers can help close existing prospects, they are most effective for generating pre-sales leads because executives and decision-makers rely on white papers when researching solutions to problems. White papers used to close a sale tend to be more technical and are usually targeted at influencers. However, hybrid papers are also effective sales closers, as they tend to address a combination of business and technical benefits.

Demonstrating thought leadership and generating leads are the most popular uses of white papers. In the *2005 White Paper Writer Industry Survey*[11], hundreds of writers indicated that they use white papers primarily to demonstrate thought leadership and secondly to generate sales leads, both of which can be accomplished in a single document.

White papers typically educate readers on a company's value proposition in a soft-sell manner. Because white papers are usually educational and not hard-sell pieces, they can quickly become viral documents that spread across an organization. A more technical white paper is often used to describe processes and help educate potential customers on how a solution operates.

Sample Application

If your company has just developed a new product that alters or enhances an existing solution in a significant way, a white paper would be appropriate. Consider a fictitious company that is about to release a voice-controlled system for managing e-mail. A white paper that explains the time necessary to type emails and how new voice solutions speed the process via dictation might be effective. The white paper could be used to either generate leads or as a sales closing tool that describes the process and how it works.

White papers can be sent as responses to advertisements or when a salesperson has engaged a prospect who is asking for more information. Kantor explains their many sales uses: "White papers are used as online collateral, as handouts to support live presentations, as e-mail

---

[11] Stelzner, M. (November 2005). *WhitePaperSource*. 2005 White paper writer industry survey: Identifying trends and issues faced by white paper writers, http://www.whitepapersource.com/report/.

attachments in business correspondence, as incentive offers within advertisements and as a core ingredient within a direct mail campaign." Willerton adds that white papers can help a company gain grass-roots support from "the techie in the back room."

White papers are most popular in the technology marketplace. However, white papers are also used in the financial services, medical and governmental market-places, among others. White papers are particularly useful among business-to-business technology compa-nies that offer complex and costly solutions.

The vast majority of white papers are distributed as electronic documents in the form of Adobe PDF files.[12] In the past, white papers were printed and mailed; however, the Internet has opened up new distribution models, dramatically reducing the need to print white papers.

White papers are often posted on corporate websites, distributed via e-mail and syndicated via a number of fee-based outlets, including Bitpipe, KnowledgeStorm and ITPapers (see Appendix III).

WHO READS WHITE PAPERS?

In the past, white papers were primarily targeted at engi-neers and technical influencers. However, today's typical white paper reader has shifted significantly. Modern white paper readers are decision-makers and tend to be businesspeople rather than engineers.

If they are targeted appropriately, white papers can be valuable to literally anyone. For example, a very small business owner or an investor are worthwhile recipi-ents of white papers—just be aware that they may be more accustomed to the term *guide* than *white paper* (a small label change like this can have a big impact on a marketing campaign).

---

[12] See http://www.adobe.com/products/acrobat/adobepdf.html for information about Adobe PDF files.

HOW HAVE WHITE PAPERS EVOLVED?

If natural selection applies to white papers, it seems that the technical white paper is becoming an endangered breed. In the 1970s, white papers were internal corporate documents that revealed strategy and tactical plans, which were referred to as *marketing requirement documents.*

By the 1980s, most white papers were very technical documents that explained processes in excruciating detail. However, businesses began to see the lead generation potential of white papers and held them out as lures to attract sales prospects.

By the mid 1990s, the marketing value of white papers began catching on in the technology world. Slowly, the predominant reader of a white paper began to shift from a technical user to a business decision-maker. Because business readers focus more on business challenges and less on the inner workings of solutions, white papers have also become significantly shorter.

Distribution is another more recent change. Today's white paper outlets, portals and electronic distribution channels were largely absent 10 years ago. In addition, many industries outside of the technology marketplace are starting to use white papers.

THE EMERGENCE OF WHITE PAPERS AS MARKETING TOOLS

How have white papers emerged as marketing tools? Prior to the 1990s, datasheets, brochures and presentations were the predominant forms of marketing collateral. These marketing tools were often perceived to be biased materials that were discounted by many prospects who were early in the decision-making process.

How could marketing professionals get their complex messages in front of qualified customers? A marketing tool was needed that would be read by potential clients and work as a sales agent before contact was ever initiated.

Many businesses were submitting contributed articles to trade publications. These articles stripped out much of the typical marketing spin and began educating readers on new technology. However, this type of marketing made businesses subject to the whim of publishers.

White papers became the solution. They were already accepted in the technology world as educational documents that described technical processes. They also had longer shelf lives than articles. In some cases, portions of the white paper could also be repurposed for contributed articles.

Analyst firms were some of the first to write business benefits white papers. For example, IDC and the Gartner Group were sources businesses could engage to have an authority write what was perceived to be an objective paper on the state of an industry. However, the high costs of having analysts produce white papers prompted many companies to begin writing their own.

Today, most organizations either use in-house or contract writers to author their white papers, rather than subject-matter experts. Regardless of who writes them, executives and decision-makers rely heavily on white papers when researching solutions to problems.

WHITE PAPER STANDARDS

Despite the fact that millions of white papers have been written, there are few or no recognized industry standards for white paper writing. I have seen one-page advertisements and full-length books wrongly labeled as white papers. The phrase is so attractive to some industries that many businesses are slapping the label on just about anything in hopes of jumping on the white paper bandwagon.

To help establish standards, WhitePaperSource surveyed hundreds of white paper writers. Here are some of the findings that resulted from their surveys and forum discussions. White papers should:

- Begin by addressing problems, challenges or needs, rather than the solution
- Range from 5 to 12 pages in length, on average
- Educate as a top priority
- Avoid direct selling
- Focus on benefits more than features
- Contain information useful to the reader
- Avoid the use of humor

Now that you understand what a white paper is, its value and how it is used, it is important to spend some time examining how to create a well-written white paper. Even though white papers are everywhere, most are never read cover-to-cover. To ensure your paper is embraced by readers, it is critical to start with a thorough needs assessment. The next chapter will reveal what you need to know to properly frame a white paper project.

✸ Chapter 2 ✸

The First Step: The Needs Assessment

A good house must be built on a firm foundation or eventually cracks will appear that produce all sorts of problems. Similarly, a white paper must be built on a solid gathering of basic facts to ensure every written word is reinforced by a clear goal and pre-approved course of action.

This chapter addresses the important first steps of producing a quality white paper and introduces a process approach to writing white papers. The chapter also explains the key steps of the needs assessment, which includes determining the topic, identifying the ideal reader and pinpointing an objective.

TEN-STEP PROCESS TO WRITING WHITE PAPERS

As with any complex project, adopting a tried and proven process model will greatly reduce the pain and agony you otherwise might experience when writing your white paper. The ten-step process outlined below came from the school of trial and error and was refined over many years. It is rather simple and straightforward at first glance. However, its grace is found in the details. Here is the mile-high view:

Step	Description
1. Clarify the topic	Focus your lens. Come to the table with a specific topic in mind. Will you be writing about a broad subject or a narrow one?
2. Identify your ideal reader	Are you fishing for whales or guppies? Identify your ideal reader with precision. Pinpoint the intended reader's industry, job title, age and general disposition. Keep the reader in mind as you write the white paper.
3. Decide on an objective	Figure out your endgame early. Do you want to educate, sell, inform or differentiate? Is this paper designed to generate leads? Will it be technical or business benefits focused? Be sure to stay on topic through the entire white paper.
4. Develop an outline	Good directions get you to your destination. An outline helps break a paper into manageable pieces and keeps you on track. Be sure to receive buy-in from key people before you write the first word.
5. Interview the experts	The best content lives in someone else's head. If you are not the sole content expert, interview other sources to gather a fresh perspective. When interviewing experts, be sure to ask probing questions such as "Why is that important?" and "What is the implication of that?"
6. Research	The web is your library. Read as much as you can about your paper's topic. Seek industry analysis, competitor information and internal documents.
7. Write the first page first	Lay the foundation and build on it. The first page sets the stage for your document. Carefully craft and refine it to perfection. The rest of your paper will build on those first words.
8. Write the title	First impressions matter. Create a relevant and compelling title that will invite readers to explore your efforts further. Keep it simple and focus on the benefits the paper will bring your ideal reader.
9. Write the core	Break the paper into manageable components. Continue to repeatedly refine, streamline, redraft and fine-tune your messaging. Come back to your paper many times over a period of days. Be sure to stay focused on your topic, your objective and your ideal reader.
10. Hire an editor	For a refining touch, seek an editor. As a painter is blind to missed spots on a wall, so too will you be blind to errors in your writing. An editor can provide an objective safety net for correcting glaring problems and can ensure your words are well-written.

Now that you are equipped with the basics, you can start formulating some ideas. Remember to keep plenty of caffeine on hand! The majority of this book will dig deep into the items outlined on the prior page.

AN INTRODUCTION TO THE NEEDS ASSESSMENT

Remember Donald Trump's hit reality show, *The Apprentice*? It was early in the first season and the men—team Versacorp—suffered a crushing defeat by the women—team Protégé. The task was to develop an ad campaign for an airline while under an extreme deadline.

Team Versacorp made a fatal error that ultimately led to their demise: they decided to forgo calling the airline to understand its needs. They sacrificed clarity for time. Versacorp chose not to ask the questions that would have produced a targeted result. The women's team did the right thing and ultimately prevailed. Skipping the needs assessment is akin to swimming blindfolded.

The essence of the needs assessment involves asking questions about the target audience and the white paper's objectives.

For example, while writing a white paper for a large mobile phone manufacturer, I determined that their primary target audience was analysts and the media, and their secondary audience was small-business users. Had I incorrectly assumed the target audience was carriers, the entire paper would have been written from the wrong perspective.

Secondly, I discovered that their objective was to convince the media that their new technology was important and worth writing about. Having that information was critical to help me develop a targeted and relevant white paper.

Here are a few needs assessment tips:

- Identify the primary and secondary target audiences.

- Ask many questions about the audience: what is their typical title, average age, general disposition and so on.
- Determine the objective of the white paper: to educate, sell, inform, differentiate, introduce, etc.
- What are the big issues, problems or needs that must be addressed in the paper?
- Develop an outline that will guide future discussions.
- Who are the key players who must be interviewed?
- Who are the key competitors to analyze?
- What is the schedule and timeline?

By understanding and agreeing up front on the direction of the paper, you will save yourself from team Versacorp's fate.

SELECTING THE TOPIC

Understanding the topical scope of the white paper early is important. If you have been tasked to write a white paper on a broad subject, it is important to drill down to specific areas of focus. For example, consider a white paper on the topic of homeland security. Some questions to ask may include:

- Will this be a high-level overview?
- Should I focus on certain aspects of homeland security, such as air travel, border security, natural resource protection, etc.?
- Will I be introducing the key benefits of homeland security?
- Will I be portraying the positive or negative aspects of homeland security?
- From whose perspective should I be examining the topic: American families, law enforcement, local government authorities, industry, etc.?

A thorough examination of the topic will help set the stage for the rest of the needs assessment process.

IDENTIFYING THE IDEAL READER

Determining who will be reading the document is an important early step when preparing to write a white paper. Often, marketing folks talk about target audience when discussing the early stages of a project. While the target audience is very important, for white papers it is essential to distinguish the target reader. By simply asking, "Who is the ideal reader of this paper?", an interesting discussion usually ensues.

When assessing the ideal reader, it is best to drive the discussion to a single reader. Pinpointing the ideal reader will help develop the outline, mature the writing and guide discussions when things get off track.

Some questions to ask that will help your discussion include:

- In what industry does this person work?
- How big is the company that employs this person?
- What is the title of this person?
- How technical is the reader?
- What are his or her job responsibilities?
- What is the reader's general disposition (busy, actively researching, etc.)?
- Is the reader generally male or female?
- How old is the reader?
- How familiar is the topic to the ideal reader?

Asking many questions to clearly define the ideal reader will not only help you bring clarity to your white paper project, it will also enhance your credibility.

It is important to submit the ideal reader along with your outline for approval to key people within the company before you begin writing. Ensuring buy-in will help you keep things focused when you continue down the path of your project.

Once you are armed with a clear picture of your ideal reader, be sure to constantly check yourself during your interviews and writing process to be certain you are collecting information and writing about topics that matter to this reader.

Frequently, ideal readers turn out to be IT directors or corporate executives. When writing to these high-level audiences, it is very important to focus more on business benefits and less on technical nuances. Similarly, if your ideal reader is a technical administrator, it is important to focus on processes, procedures and details that matter to these readers. Building a business case for a technical audience is less appropriate because these types of readers are usually influencers rather than decision-makers.

You will find yourself in situations where the people you are interviewing are telling you to write about topics that seem misguided based on what you understand about the ideal reader. When this occurs, a simple way to get things back on track is to ask, "Why is this important to our ideal reader?" Frequently, silence will be the result, along with a confession that this may be off track. Another important tip is to start every interview by clearly stating who the ideal reader is.

When your reader is clearly identified, you will always have a beacon to navigate by when your writing goes astray.

Examples of Ideal Readers
Here are some ideal readers from actual white papers:
- Manager or director of information security for $750 million or larger enterprise that handles transactions online, such as a financial services or large e-commerce organization.
- Portfolio managers or chief financial officers at small- to medium-sized depositories such as

(continued)

banks, credit unions or thrifts; typically male, aged 30 to 50.
- Very small business owners, such as a family businesses, eBay businesses, contractors or hobbyists.
- IT director or chief information officer for organizations with 100 or more mobile workers who are mostly located in the field.
- Marketing directors at Latin American mobile phone operators.

SECONDARY READERS

Often, white papers will be targeted at more than one group of readers or the paper will typically work its way to the ideal reader via a gatekeeper. When there is a secondary target reader, it is appropriate to ask the same questions about this reader, as described in the previous section.

You should discern whether the differences between the ideal and the secondary readers are so opposite that they will result in a weak white paper. For example, consider a white paper that is targeted primarily at chief technical officers (CTOs) and database administrators as a secondary target. By asking many questions, your assessment should reveal that CTOs care about high-level business concerns such as increasing productivity and reducing costs, and administrators care about the technical details and inner workings of a solution. When primary and secondary audiences have very dissimilar interests, the paper will not grab the attention of either reader very well. If it turns out that the paper is primarily targeted at CTOs, then consider creating a second paper that meets the needs of administrators.

DETERMINING THE OBJECTIVE

Start with the end in mind. When writing white papers, it is critical to identify a clear objective. Objectives come in many flavors, including overt and covert objectives. *Overt objectives* are the goals you would not mind sharing with the world. However, *covert objectives* are the secret goals you hope to achieve with your white paper. Below are some examples.

Overt Goals	Covert Goals
Educate our customers on the value of our technology	Knock our bigger competition off its pedestal
Establish thought leadership in our category	Beat everyone to the market with our idea and develop the solution as we go
Describe the business advantages of our solution	Generate qualified leads for our sales team

Most overt white paper goals involve educating, selling, informing or differentiating a company, product or service. Covert goals typically include attacking the competition, gaining a first-to-market position or generating leads.

It is also important to determine if the paper will be technical, business benefits focused or a hybrid paper (see Chapter 1 for details). Understanding how the paper will be used is also helpful. For example, will it be part of an advertising campaign, used as a sales follow-up tool or groomed for a contributed article in a trade publication?

Be sure to check your work against the white paper's goals. For example, consider an overt goal of objectively educating your readers on the value of your technology. If you do not properly define terms or lay out a solid case that proves there are emerging market trends that justify the need, you may not be truly educating your readers.

By clearly defining the objective of the white paper, you will have a map to fall back on when your writing goes astray and a litmus test to determine if your written words are in line with the goals of the white paper.

The needs assessment represents the beginning of a well-thought-out plan. It identifies the topic of your white paper, your ideal reader and the objective. With this important information, you can begin the process of establishing an outline. The next chapter will review the core elements of an outline and provide some useful examples.

✳ Chapter 3 ✳

White Paper Outlines

"'Begin at the beginning,' the King said, gravely, 'and go on till you come to the end; then stop.'"

—Lewis Carroll, *Alice's Adventures in Wonderland* (1865).

T he outline is both the beginning of your white paper journey and your map to the end. Follow the agreed upon path and your destination will be clear. Perhaps the most important part of the white paper process is developing a compelling outline and obtaining the appropriate approvals before setting pen to paper or fingers to keyboard.

Think of the outline as an architectural blueprint that guides the development of your paper. This chapter will focus on different approaches to white paper outlines, present possible content sections and provide practical examples.

READER-FOCUSED WHITE PAPERS

When writing the outline, you need to come to the table with a general white paper approach. There are two primary ways to write white papers: (1) by focusing on your self-interests or (2) by concentrating on the interests of your readers. The self-interest approach focuses *exclusively* on a product, service or solution by expounding on its benefits, features and implications. While effective in some circumstances, this approach is best used in something other than a white paper, such as a data sheet or product brief.

The self-serving approach is often focused on the mistaken belief that people like to read details about why your product is the best thing since the invention of the Internet. This method is an ineffective approach to writing that turns many readers off immediately.

If you want prospects and customers to actually read the paper, you should try to gain affinity with them right away. It should be noted that it is perfectly appropriate to touch on features and benefits if they are carefully crafted into the white paper.

The alternative approach, and the one I strongly recommend, is to focus on the needs of your readers. This can be effectively accomplished by leading with the problems your solution overcomes, rather than the actual solution itself. To many people, this seems counterintuitive, but it really is just the opposite. *By focusing on the pain points experienced by the reader and talking about the problems caused by those pains, you are establishing credibility with the reader and simultaneously filtering out unqualified customers.*

Consider the two examples in the box on the next page. Example A mentions the problem, but it is tainted by self-serving references to the company and the product. Contrast that with Example B, which focuses exclusively on the problem and hints at the solution in a broad sense.

Readers will feel more inclined to read Example B because it seems more educational to them. They have the chance to learn about a new technology that could solve their problem. With Example A, they learn more about the company and the product and less about the solution. Readers of Example A may never get to the point where they understand what the solution is. By describing problems, you are really developing an important affinity with readers.

EXAMPLE A:
Title: Groundbreaking TechWidget by XYZ Company Solves Time Management Dilemma!
Opening Sentence: XYZ Company has done it again! Another great TechWidget invention can help you overcome time management challenges.

EXAMPLE B:
Title: Solving the Time Management Dilemma with Technology
Opening Sentence: If you find it difficult to manage your time effectively, a new class of technology products may be the solution you are looking for.

You can take it a step further by looking at issues such as historical precedence, describing new classes of solutions that address the problems and even identifying what to look for in a solution, while never once mentioning your product name or company (at least not yet). This altruistic approach will score major points with the reader and greatly increase the likelihood he or she will actually read the entire paper.

What Type of Writer Are You? Wisdom From the Lord of the Rings
During your journey as a writer, projects may have provided you beautiful and safe Rivendell-type opportunities. If you are experienced, you have also stumbled into the dark, dangerous and unfamiliar

(continued)

Helm's Deep. Perhaps your journey is just beginning or you are well on your way, but the destination is unclear. Are you an "Aragorn," "Legolas" or "Frodo" writer? Each has a unique style and advantages suited to specific types of writing. Much can be learned from J.R.R. Tolkien's epic *The Lord of the Rings* characters.

Aragorn: Writing for kings: The leader of the Rangers and the future king of Gondor, Aragorn is a knowledgeable warrior, pathfinder and healer. Able to focus on big issues and leadership, an "Aragorn" writer looks at the big picture and focuses on challenges that are relevant to leaders. The "Aragorn" writer avoids features and technical discussions while focusing on problems, benefits and implications. If you are "Aragorn," you speak a language that is easy to understand and get to the heart of critical matters quickly.

Legolas: Writing with precision: Legolas, an elf, is fast, calculating and possesses incredible vision. He is always the first to draw an arrow in battle and knows how to thread his way through the most treacherous forests, noiseless and unseen. "Legolas is a scout, a hunter, a woodland elf, with deep personal connections to the natural world, but not to the policies, lore, history and problems of the lords and stewards of his race."[1] The "Legolas" writer is one who demonstrates how things work in detail. If you are a "Legolas" writer, you are able to transcribe the most technical processes with a keen ability to convey the innermost workings of any topic.

(continued)

---

[1] Brundige, B. Legolas of Mirkwood: Prince among equals, http://www.istad.org/tolkien/legolas.html.

Frodo: Writing to bridge worlds: Frodo, a hobbit, was chosen to step outside the comfort of the Shire and into very foreign places that required an open, sharp mind. When encountering other races, Frodo tries to speak their languages and observe their customs. His uncle, Bilbo Baggins, reminded him, "You step into the Road, and if you don't keep your feet, there is no knowing where you might be swept off to." The "Frodo" writer lives in both the world of Aragorn and the world of Legolas. Able to bridge technical concepts and higher-level benefits, the "Frodo" writer is able to address the how and the why. If you are a "Frodo" writer, not only do you speak and translate technical processes, you can understand and convey higher-level benefits.

OUTLINE INGREDIENTS

The goal of most white papers is to gracefully lead the reader toward the conclusion that your product or service will best meet his or her needs. To accomplish this, you must substantially make your case.

Adopting the problem-solution approach to writing white papers is a very successful model. Simply stated, *by leading with some challenges faced by your readers and suggesting how to solve their problems, you can develop a compelling white paper that engages readers.*

As a good salad has the proper mix of greens, vegetables, meat and spices, so must a good white paper contain a balance of different ingredients to appeal to the taste of your readers. Here are a few areas that may help you add substance to your outline:

The Greens: Core Elements of Most White Papers

A good white paper will include many of these five basic elements: (1) a challenge, problem or need, (2) a solution, (3) the benefits of the solution, (4) a list of considerations when examining a solution and (5) the specific advantages of your product or service. What follows is a brief explanation of each of these essential elements.

Problem: Often, white papers lead with challenges faced by the ideal reader. By discussing problems faced by your reader and the implications of not dealing with those challenges, you set up an opportunity to reaffirm the reader's concerns and reveal new issues that may not have been considered. The goal of discussing challenges is to build affinity with your readers.

Solution: The next logical step after laying out a challenge is to introduce the solution. Solutions can be generic or specific. For example, push-to-talk technology may be a generic solution to improving field worker communication. The Nextel network may be a specific solution. If the paper is educational in nature, introduce the generic solution before the specific solution to remove the appearance of salesmanship.

Benefits: A good discussion around the benefits of a solution is always a useful addition to a white paper. The benefits should be directly related to the problems you put forth. For example, if your problem is that employees are spending too much time surfing the web and you have introduced a tracking solution that monitors employee surfing habits, a benefit might be, "Deters employees from viewing inappropriate web content." Benefits should be mentioned in a solution-agnostic manner.

The "What to Look for" Pitch: An overview of important considerations when seeking a solution is an effective way to add substance to a white paper. This section of your paper can be "the buyer's guide" that helps your readers set up a standard by which all of your competitors will be judged. This is a great opportunity for you to toot your own horn and get away with it. For example, you might state that it is important to work with a company that has an established client base and a global support team. You could explain these benefits and ultimately knock your smaller competitors out of the equation for the reader. This should all be done at a high level without getting into the specifics regarding your company or product. It is useful to note that you can focus on both corporate and solution-specific items on your list.

Specific Advantages: After a generic solution has been explained, it may make sense to clarify the specific advantages your product or service brings to the market. There is a slight distinction between benefits and specific advantages. Benefits should be generic to the solution and specific advantages should be highly related to your product or service. For example, if your paper is discussing the advantages of training employees to be accountable in the workplace, a benefit might include a statement such as, "Individuals display a willingness to answer for the results of their actions." A specific advantage of your training program might be, "XYZ solution includes metrics for measuring employee acceptance of accountability."

The Flavor: Additional Outline Topics

If you want to take your white paper beyond the basics, there are many additional sections that can be added to augment some of the core elements outlined above. The following list is not exhaustive and not all of these topics are appropriate for any single white paper.

Market Drivers: A persuasive white paper might reveal a need by building a solid market driver or trends section. Market trends tend to be used early in the white paper to demonstrate the key market movements that justify examining a solution in detail. For example, a white paper on network security might examine the number of recent network attacks and cite specific analyst research that predicts a future, increased need. Whenever possible, market trends should reference third-party research.

Historical Overview: A historical overview can be a powerful addition to your white paper. In the world of technology, it's useful to discuss what has led to the modern-day dilemma addressed by your solution. Take, for example, the topic of multimodality. Briefly, this new technology allows mobile callers to talk on their cell phones and simultaneously interact with the onscreen display. A historical overview section could focus on how consumers have moved from touchtone dialing to text messaging to mobile applications and ultimately to converging next-generation solutions. The objective is to show how the needs of users have evolved and to set the stage for your new technology.

How It Works: If your paper is technical or on a process-related topic, a section describing how your product works may be in order. Diagrams can be used to augment your writing and can visually convey the steps or components involved with a solution. For example, if you are writing about how hosted e-mail services are ideal for eliminating spam, it may make sense to create a section that demonstrates how the model works.

Examples: It is always useful to explain situations where your solution would be particularly effective. You can be as specific or as generic as you like. Sometimes it is helpful to talk about specific industries where the solution works well. Other times it makes sense to talk about specific customers who have found success with the product.

Tips: If you are writing a white paper that is educational in nature, it may make sense to include a section on tips or pitfalls to avoid. Some examples might include ten tips when hiring a subcontractor or what to avoid when incorporating. These tips can be treated as sidebar material or integrated into the paper.

Comparisons: For some white papers, doing side-by-side comparisons of two options, or the pros and cons of a product or service may be appropriate. This can be a useful tool to quickly identify the advantages of one product over another.

Features: Features belong mostly in documents other than white papers, such as brochures and data-sheets. However, when implications are added to the list of features, they may be appropriate for some white papers. For example, if your product features easy-to-use wizards, an implication might be a boost in productivity by offloading technical experts. Features may also be discussed in a technical white paper. Features are best conveyed in a table or a bulleted list.

A New Class of Products: You may need to write about something that has never been addressed in the unique way you need to address it. In these circumstances, it may make sense to introduce your solution as part of a new class of products. This can be very powerful because you have an opportunity not only to name the class, but to define its key characteristics. For example, one of my clients developed automated software that responds to emails using artificial intelligence, which in turn offloads support staff. We coined the term *virtual support teams* and it stuck in the industry. When you create a new class of products, you can refer to the benefits of the class and even address specific minimum requirements for a product to be part of the class.

Be sure to examine Chapter 8 for an in-depth examination of many of the possibilities addressed above.

OUTLINE TEMPLATES

What follows are some proven white paper outlines that you can apply to almost any type of white paper. These outlines can serve as templates for writing your white paper and help guide you throughout the entire process, from interviews to writing.

Standard Business Benefits Paper

The following outline is appropriate for a 6- to 10-page white paper that is educational in nature and focused on business benefits.

> **Introduction**: Introduce the high-level problem and the high-level solution in the first few paragraphs
> **Market Drivers**: Discuss what is driving the market toward your solution
> **Problems**: Identify the top 3 to 5 issues related to the high-level problem
> **Generic Solution**: Introduce the solution in a generic way
> • **Define**: Clearly define the solution
> • **Benefits**: Explain how it overcomes the problems listed earlier
> • **What to Look for**: List top 10 considerations when looking for a solution
> **Specific Solution**: Discuss the specific advantages of your product, service or solution
> **Call to Action**: Provide a logical next step and include company contact information

The standard business benefits white paper starts with a quick introduction of the problem and solution faced by your ideal reader. The market drivers discussion examines trends in the market that reveal a need. This section can be placed before or after the problems section depending on where it best fits. Sometimes market drivers are meant to pull a reader into the paper and other times they work well as a transition to the solution. The problems section should address the challenges faced by your ideal reader when he or she does not have a solution similar to yours in place.

When introducing the solution, it is best to use generic concepts. Rather than mentioning your product name, introduce the category it falls in. For example, rather than "Motorola's Bluetooth Car Kit," lead with something like "wireless automotive solutions." When defining a solution and discussing its benefits, remain category-focused rather than product-focused. Thus, examine the key components of your generic solution and how it helps overcome the identified problems.

The "what to look for" list should focus on key considerations when seeking a solution. The specific solution should only touch on the high-level advantages of your solution, rather than hitting the reader over the head with excessive details that belong in a different document. The conclusion should include a clear call to action, such as a web address that readers can visit for additional information.

Longer Business Benefits or Hybrid Paper

The following outline is appropriate for a 9- to 15-page white paper that is educational in nature, focused on business benefits and that provides some technical details.

Introduction: Introduce the high-level problem and the high-level solution in the first few paragraphs

Market Drivers: Discuss what is driving the market toward your solution

Problems: Identify the top 3 to 5 issues related to the high-level problem

Historical Approach: Talk about how challenges have historically been addressed

Generic Solution: Introduce the solution in a generic way

- **Define**: Clearly define the solution
- **Benefits**: Explain how it overcomes the problems listed earlier
- **What to Look for**: List top 10 considerations when looking for a solution
- **How It Works**: Describe how the solution works or its process

- **Examples**: Provide some case studies or hypothetical examples

Specific Solution: Discuss the specific advantages
of your product, service or solution

Call to Action: Provide a logical next step and
include company contact information

Three key elements were added to this outline that take
it beyond the standard business benefits white paper: the
historical discussion, how it works and examples. Not
only does this increase the length of the white paper, it
provides a bit more technical depth than a standard business benefits white paper.

The historical approach is very helpful when your solution takes existing products to the next level of evolution.
For example, if you are writing about laptop computer
security, you might want to talk about how security has
evolved from simple password protection to integrated
thumbprint readers. When discussing how things work,
it is often helpful to describe processes and enhance the
section with diagrams.

When providing examples, consider sticking with hypothetical applications of your solution to avoid the need
for legal approval from customers, which is typical when
disclosing details about a specific company. For example,
if Microsoft is your customer, you might say, "A leading
software developer achieved significant benefits…"

Technical Paper

A technical white paper is usually focused on describing
a process or procedure. The problem-solution approach
can still work well for technical papers. Here is a sample
outline that would be very effective for a technical white
paper:

Introduction: Introduce the technology
Market Drivers: Discuss the challenges that are
driving the need for your technology

Historical Approach: Talk about how technical challenges historically have been addressed
Specific Solution: Discuss the specifics of the process or technology
- **Define**: Clearly define the technology
- **Benefits**: Explain how it overcomes the problems listed earlier
- **How It Works**: Describe how the solution works
- **Applications**: Illustrate how the technology could be applied
- **Key Features**: Discuss some of the major features
- **Comparisons With Alternatives**: Discuss the competitive advantages to alternate technology
Conclusion/Call to Action: Summarize the paper topics and include company contact information

The above outline would be appropriate for a rather large technical white paper. For a smaller white paper, consider removing the historical approach, comparison with alternatives and applications. A technical white paper places the problems portion of the discussion in the market drivers section. There is also no need to generically introduce the solution in a technical white paper. This type of paper is usually used after a sales engagement has begun with a prospective client, meaning clients are in the analysis stage with your specific solution. The "How It Works" and "Features" sections of a technical white paper are typically a very large part of the paper.

GETTING APPROVALS

Once you have developed the outline, an important next step is to assure the appropriate people approve it before you begin interviewing or writing.

Often, the person who is your primary interface or project lead is not in a position to approve the direction of your paper. For freelance writers, the marketing communications manager is usually the internal champion for white paper projects. However, it is typically a product line manager or vice president of the company who has requested the white paper be created. It is critical that these key people have a chance to approve the target audience, objective and outline prior to your performing any additional work.

Getting critical buy-in early is important to reduce the likelihood of surprises later in the project. For example, if the CEO has approved the outline and later decides the approach should be changed once a draft has been written, remind your key contacts that the direction was blessed before you began writing. If you are an outside contractor, this is your opportunity to explain that a scope change will incur extra expenses.

This chapter introduced the value of reader-focused white papers and the core elements of most white paper outlines. Once the outline has been developed and approved, the next step is to begin asking many questions. The next chapter will reveal the value of interviewing and introduce many tactics to improve the results of your discussions.

✳ Chapter 4 ✳

Interviewing

Do you like chicken? Why do you like chicken? Tell me three ways you like your chicken prepared?

You've just been peppered with interview questions. As you answer them, you will see that some elicit more information than others.

The goal of this chapter is to introduce you to the art of interviewing, discuss why it is critical when writing white papers and provide some specific examples that will help you with your white paper projects.

WHY INTERVIEWING?

Perhaps one of the bigger challenges faced by white paper writers is coming up with good content. The default course of action is to do a web search and see what someone else has written on a topic (more on that in Chapter 5). While this approach can yield valuable information, the best pearls reside inside someone else's head.

An extensive study by research group IDC revealed that information workers spend more than 27 hours a week searching, gathering and analyzing information.[1] If business professionals spend so much time seeking and analyzing data, why wouldn't you leverage their expertise and save yourself the search effort? The challenge is getting directly to what matters inside the heads of others.

What is the solution? It is very simple. Start asking direct questions. The key to peeking inside another person's brain is to ask laser-focused questions.

Here are some reasons we avoid asking questions:

- We hate asking for directions
- We think we know it all
- We do not want to look stupid
- We do not know who to ask
- We do not know what to ask

Interestingly, an extensive study of hundreds of white paper writers found that nearly 70 percent of writers spend between zero and 5 hours performing interviews when writing an average white paper.[2] In addition, fewer than 1 in 5 found interviews to be difficult or very difficult. Although interviewing is perceived to be easy, white paper writers are not fully utilizing the power of interviews, as evidenced by the small amount of time allocated to interviewing.

My three-year-old daughter is already a well-practiced interviewer. She recently asked me, "Daddy, why do we have bones?" I answered, "If we didn't have bones we wouldn't be able to walk. Bones keep everything in place." She seemed satisfied by the answer.

Kids seem to be very good at asking the "why" questions. However, as adults, we often avoid such basic questions.

---

[1] Feldmen, S., et al. (March 2005). The hidden costs of information work, http://www.factiva.com/factivaforum/2005/frankfurt/TheHiddenCostsOfInformationWork.pdf.
[2] Stelzner, M. (November 2005). *WhitePaperSource.* 2005 White paper writer industry survey: Identifying trends and issues faced by white paper writers, http://www.whitepapersource.com/report/.

Here are some reasons why performing interviews is important for white paper projects:

- Asking an expert a good question speeds the research process
- Experts often have access to information that you could never otherwise find
- Interviewing is more fun than simply searching the Internet
- Some of the best content will come from an interview

Now that the case has been made that you should interview more, let's examine interviewing in more detail.

THE ART OF INTERVIEWING

Regardless of the field, a white paper writer should conduct interviews, and the best "content-rich" interviews are with the experts: the chief scientists, product managers, engineers and inventors who spawned the product or idea you need to write about.

Your task is to crack open the right minds and extract the valuable content you need for your white paper. Someone inside your company or at the client site has the critical information you are looking for.

Let's examine different types of questions:

Bad question: Is a data backup plan important?
Better question: Why is a data backup plan important?
Great question: Can you tell me three reasons why a backup plan is important?
Excellent question: What are the implications of not having a backup plan?

The first step is to ask questions that will elicit the types of responses you are hoping for. Avoid questions that can be answered with a simple yes or no. Very broad questions will return very broad responses. What makes a question great or excellent are its specifics. Asking for three examples or the implication of something will cause someone to really think about a question and the results are often shiny pearls of knowledge.

Here are some great follow-up questions to ask when you accidentally put forward a bad question in an interview, or if the response is bland:

- Can you please elaborate?
- What are some examples?
- Why does that matter?
- What is the implication to our ideal reader?
- Can you say that another way?
- How would you explain that to a non-technical person?

If you do not fully understand the answer or feel the response to your question is missing something, repeat what you just heard out loud, "So what I hear you saying is ..." This will usually bring out further discussion and clarification.

When asking questions related to a list of items such as the top benefits of a product, it is helpful to ask these types of questions, repeatedly:

- Can you provide another example?
- Are there any last topics worth mentioning?
- Can you think of anything else?
- Are we forgetting anything important?

A key is to remain silent and not attempt to put words in the mouth of the person you are interviewing. Give your expert time to think. For some of us, this is really difficult. However, try not to lead your interview subject toward an answer you have preconceived.

The Wrong Person
Sometimes it becomes obvious that the person you are interviewing is not the topical expert. It is important to ask who else should be interviewed. You may even specifically state, "Is there another subject matter expert you would recommend I speak to?" Tapping the right brains and asking pointed questions are critical to finding the valuable gems that will provide precious content for your white paper.

SETTING UP INTERVIEWS

The previous chapter talked about the importance of preparing an outline. The outline is also very foundational to setting up interviews. Once you have an approved outline, it makes sense to set up interviews for key topics of the outline. Let's take the following outline and discuss possible interviews that might result from it.

Sample Outline
- High-level problem: Poor accountability in the workforce
- High-level solution: Create a culture of accountability across the enterprise
- Problems expanded: The results of improper accountability
  - Eroding margins
  - High turnover of employees
  - Low product or service quality
- Historical approaches to accountability
- Solution: accountability training
  - Define
  - Benefits
  - Hypothetical example
  - What to look for in a training vendor
- XYZ Company solution advantages

The next step is to identify sections of the outline that can be grouped into conference calls or meetings. Based on the above outline, five separate interviews could be conducted, as follows:

Possible Interviews
- Problem: 60-90 minutes
- History: 30-60 minutes
- Solution 1 (define/benefits): 60 minutes
- Solution 2 (example/what to look for): 60 minutes
- XYZ Company Advantages: 60 minutes

The amount of time it takes to conduct specific discussions depends on your skill and the people involved. Discussions about problems can be lengthy and often disagreement and debate occur. In addition, the solution meeting is often best split into multiple discussions.

Whenever possible, keep discussions under 90 minutes to help you avoid burnout and respect the time of the experts you are interviewing. Spread the meetings over a period of days or weeks. This allows you time to digest the content of the interviews and review any documents that might be sent to you based on the discussion.

Lastly, it is important to try to keep the meetings in the same order as the outline. This helps build a foundation of knowledge for the later discussions. Keeping the meetings in order can be problematic when you are limited by content expert availability. Keep in mind that if you do not fully understand and work out the problems before you start talking about the solution, you will lack context.

After the key interview topics are identified, the next step is to invite the appropriate people to each meeting. Different types of people are appropriate for different kinds of topics. For example, a discussion about what to look for in a solution might be ideal for a salesperson who best understands the key competitive advantages of your solution.

INTERVIEWING LARGE GROUPS OF PEOPLE

When you are working on a project that has many different people who must be interviewed, you may be inclined to go through the entire outline with each person in a one-on-one call or meeting. Avoid that approach. The result will often lack depth and content experts easily can become bored talking about topics not related to their expertise.

Alternatively, conduct group conference calls or meetings to discuss key topics of the outline. Assign key experts to meetings based on their expertise.

If a specific discussion involves three or more experts, you most likely will have one or two dominate the discussion or you will have a very long call. Your task will be to draw out the other experts who are not talking and ask their opinions. It often makes sense to extend the length of a meeting or schedule a follow-up call if you did not accomplish everything you expected.

A key advantage to group discussions is that people often spawn ideas and thoughts from others in the meeting, or strike down comments that are not relevant to your paper.

STARTING AND RECORDING THE INTERVIEW

When you start an interview, be sure to properly "set the stage." Setting the stage essentially involves beginning the interview by focusing everyone on the topic at hand. Begin with a brief overview of the ideal reader, the topic, the objective and a review of the portions of outline related to the call. Also, state the duration of the meeting and specify what you hope to achieve by the end of the discussion. It is important to set the stage every time you conduct an interview, even if you are interviewing the same people each time. This step helps focus the interview and redirects the discussion when it veers off on a tangent. When people join a group interview late, it is appropriate to quickly bring them up to speed by setting the stage for them as well.

A critical part of the interview involves documenting the important information that comes from the minds of your experts. Taking notes can be a painful process. This brings me back to my college days when I used to write feverishly while professors would talk faster than I could record. Despite the amazing technology that exists today, I still resort to pen and paper to document the interviews I conduct. Sometimes this gets a bit challenging when my interviewees talk very fast or about topics that are beyond my immediate comprehension.

Many of my colleagues use a variety of techniques to record conference calls, as follows:

Good Old-Fashioned Tape Recorder

Tape recorders work fairly well in a conference room setting. However, when conducting a conference call, it is a bit trickier. Radio Shack sells an interface that connects the phone to the tape recorder, enabling you to easily record the content of a call.[3] It should be noted that in the United States you must inform everyone that you will be recording the call and receive their consent. It is also advisable to take notes during the call in case some of the recording is not audible. If the recorder has a counter, jot down the number during the critical points of the call so you can quickly go back and review.

---

[3] See Smart Phone Recorder Control, Catalog #43-2208.

Phone to Computer

Some nifty technology devices allow you to bypass the traditional recorder and store discussions directly to a computer. JK Audio sells a product that allows the phone to be connected to the audio card inside your PC.[4] Griffin Technology sells a product called iMic that allows you to connect the low-tech Radio Shack device discussed in the previous section to your computer via its USB port.[5]

Finally, software is required to record the audio and save it. It is useful to keep an eye on the recording time counter if a topic was discussed that requires further review, so you can revisit it later.

Microsoft Word's notebook layout feature is a useful audio capture tool, especially if you take notes by typing. This handy feature allows you to record the discussion and type notes at the same time. As you type, your notes are time-stamped so you can instantly replay the audio by simply clicking a little speaker icon next to your line of notes. When you save the document, your notes and the audio are saved in one convenient file.

If you want the recording to be converted to a transcript, there are no currently available software applications that can reliably perform this task. However, there are folks who do this for a living, such as Verbatimit.com. When hiring someone to transcribe audio, you simply e-mail them the audio file and receive back the transcript a few days later.

KEEPING EXPERT INTERVIEWS FOCUSED

Ever had this conversation with a person you are trying to interview?

> **Writer**: Hi, thanks for taking time from your busy day to discuss this white paper.

---

[4] See Voice Path solution at http://www.jkaudio.com.
[5] See iMic product at http://www.griffintechnology.com.

> **Content Expert**: No problem. Before we start, I think it is important that you understand my product positioning. I would like to go through this 100-slide technical presentation with you.
> **Writer**: Umm, okay. [50 minutes later]
> **Content Expert**: I am out of time and need to run to another meeting.

You have entered the lair of the beast and are caught in a web of distraction. To escape with your treasure—the right stuff—you need to be skilled at the art of focus.

Why are content experts so hard to interview? The answer is really simple: They live in a different world. Not only do they speak a different language, often techno-gabble, they are not used to speaking with your "type"—the writer. They often cannot answer your questions in a language you can understand or they decide their agenda should be the purpose of the interview.

How do you keep the expert on task and walk away with the white paper gems?

Here are some practical steps to help guide the conversation when it wanders down the rabbit trail:

- Be sure to have a "preapproved" outline and use it to drive the interview. Remind the expert that you have approved direction and that you would like to focus on the outline.
- Be prepared before the call. Review existing documents so you can track with the expert.
- If you are nervous, do not go it alone. If you work with a marketing communications or project manager, ask him or her to join you on the call. This person can help keep focus and usually knows the expert.
- When confused, ask questions such as, "Can you give me an example?"
- When features are discussed that are too technical, ask, "What are the benefits and implications of that?"

- When you feel the discussion is going in the wrong direction, ask, "Can you explain that in terms the ideal reader of this paper would understand?" or "Do you want that information in the white paper?"

These are a few tried-and-true tips that will help you get the gold so you can get on with the paper.

This chapter discussed the value of interviews, the right way to ask questions, how to set up interviews and tips for dealing with experts. Interviews represent an excellent source of content for your white paper. After you have conducted your interviews, research will add more background material to your knowledge base. The following chapter will introduce some excellent ways to find valuable information through research.

✳ Chapter 5 ✳

Researching

"If we knew what it was we were doing, it would not be called research, would it?"

—Albert Einstein

Many of the most innovative companies in the world focus heavily on research and development. From their hard work come amazing advancements. Similarly, doing just a little digging can result in some excellent knowledge nuggets that can add flavor to your white paper.

Research is an important process that can significantly enhance the strength of your white paper and is not as difficult as you might think. According to a comprehensive study of the white paper writing process, most white paper writers think research is relatively easy.[1] However, research can be rather time-consuming. The same study revealed that white paper writers spend the most time researching (more so than writing, interviewing or editing) and that the majority of writers spend 11 or more

---

[1] Stelzner, M. (November 2005). *WhitePaperSource*. 2005 White paper writer industry survey: Identifying trends and issues faced by white paper writers, http://www.whitepapersource.com/report/.

hours conducting research for a single white paper. This chapter aims to help you speed up the research process.

The fruits of your research may reveal what others are saying about your topic or provide strong proof points for specific sections of your white paper, such as the problem, market drivers and historical overview sections. This chapter will focus predominately on how to find important information using the Internet.

USING GOOGLE FOR RESEARCH

As a writer, there is undoubtedly no better tool for researching than Google.com. What you may not realize is how much this apparently minimalist resource can accomplish.

For example, Google can search a website for a specific article. Let's say you recall seeing something in *Network World* magazine on RSS feeds, but you cannot locate it within the site's search engine. Use Google and simply type "RSS site:networkworld.com" and up come all the articles from the site containing the acronym RSS. Interestingly, a search for RSS on networkworld.com returned 237 choices and Google returned more than 300,000!

You can further restrict the results by limiting listings to those that have RSS in their title or web address. For limiting the search to titles, your search would be "intitle:RSS site:networkworld.com" or "inurl:RSS site: networkworld.com" for searches in web addresses. This is particularly useful because when a web address or title includes your keyword, there is a greater likelihood that the page content is highly related to your search.

One more interesting feature is the ability to restrict searches by date. For example, to search for articles in June 2006, try "RSS date: June 2006 site: networkworld.com." (Note that a space must exist after "date:" and before your keywords, unlike the other Google commands.) The date feature is also a bit tricky because Google simply searches for the presence of those dates anywhere on the page. Thus, 06/06, 06/2006 and June 2006 all produce different results.

One of the not-so-obvious features of Google is its dictionary. Enter almost any word or acronym and you will instantly find many definitions. For example, "define:RSS" returns more than a dozen meanings of the acronym RSS in microseconds. This is very handy when you come across an unfamiliar term or acronym that does not exist in a traditional dictionary.

Shortcuts With Google Cache

One of Google's most useful features is its cached version of results. When researching, this comes in very handy for a few key reasons. First, Google delivers content much faster than most websites, and second, Google will highlight the keywords in your search, greatly speeding your research. Here is a secret: pages that require you to register to read an article often give Google a free pass, allowing you to immediately see the content by simply looking at Google's cached copy.

To see Google's cache of a search result, simply click on the word "Cached" next to a search result listing. Notice that Google keywords are instantly highlighted on the screen. This saves you the time of scanning the page and determining if it is relevant. This is particularly handy on very long pages and lets you quickly scroll down to relevant sections of a page.

A nifty trick is the ability to highlight additional keywords on a cached page. To accomplish this, simply go to the place in your web browser where the URL is displayed and look for your keyword, such as "RSS." When you find it, simply add a plus and any keyword (i.e., "+feeds") directly after the keyword and hit return. Now, your additional keyword will also be highlighted on the page, in a unique color from other keywords.

Finding Analyst Research

Big analyst firms such as IDC, Gartner and Forrester often charge thousands of dollars for access their research reports. However, the juiciest findings are typically concentrated down to only a sentence or two.

With Google, you can find valuable analyst research on many topics quickly and at no cost. If we stick with our existing RSS topic, searching for what analysts are saying about RSS is easy. Start with a search for "IDC RSS" and you will find some of IDC's perspective on the technology.

By adding the words "outlook," "forecast," "trends," "statistics" or "growth," you will find even more focused results. Placing the words "RSS" and "trends" in quotations together (i.e., "RSS trends") will look for those two words only when they occur right next to each other, further narrowing your search. Now try repeating the same search with different analysts and you will quickly have good access to the professionals' opinions on any topic. You can also perform a search of the analysts' websites using Google, often producing press releases that summarize research findings.

Other Google Tips and Resources

Here are few lesser-known search tips for using Google:

- **The asterisk**: "computer * memory" returns only results where the words "computer" and "memory" are separated by one or more words.
- **Info**: "info:whitepapersource.com" returns detailed information about a website.
- **Case**: Keyword searches are NOT case sensitive.
- **Singular versus plural**: The words "white paper" and "white papers" produce different results. Be sure to experiment with singular and plural uses of words.
- **Short words**: Common short words, such as "or," "and," "in," "it" and "the" are ignored by Google.

Google has a number of different search-related tools that are also worth examining:

- **news.google.com**: Searches only recent news from major news sources, typically over the last 30 days.
- **www.google.com/advanced_search**: Allows refined searches.
- **books.google.com**: Searches the content of a wide range of books and reveals the actual highlighted pages on the screen.
- **scholar.google.com**: Searches scholarly and academic publications.
- **groups.google.com**: Searches newsgroup content.
- **www.google.com/unclesam**: Searches U.S. government sites only.
- **directory.google.com**: Provides a yellow pages–type listing of websites.
- **answers.google.com**: Allows you to bid a small price to have a question answered.

Now that you have a better understanding of the power of Google, be sure to use it to enhance your research, strengthen your arguments and create better white papers.

OTHER DATA SOURCES

Beyond Google there is a wealth of information available on nearly any topic, if you know where to look and who to ask.

Eyeing the Competition

Examining the competition is an excellent research strategy. You will find good information in competitors' press releases, white papers and on their web pages.

This is useful for a few reasons. First, you want to be sure the end result of your white paper addresses or debunks the messages of the competition. Second, competitors often have already done much research and you can reference the same sources when making your arguments, saving you time and effort.

Analyzing Existing Documents

Ask for anything and everything available, so you can best understand the topic. Often, even the smallest companies have a variety of resources that would be useful for a white paper. Below are a few examples of things to ask for:

- **Presentations**: PowerPoint presentations are often an excellent source of data. Be sure to examine speaker notes for additional content.
- **Analyst reports**: Often, some of the best data resides in analyst reports. However, you may need to dig through some broad reports to find something valuable for your project. Look for key statistics, possible graphics and sound bites to use in your white paper. If the reports are available in PDF format, be sure to use Acrobat Reader's search capability to speed your examination.
- **Other white papers**: Other white papers written on the same or related topics can be very valuable. Usually the first few pages of white papers will include some market assessment or analysis of the need that can prove valuable. It is also worthwhile to examine footnotes and references to see if you can find additional information. See Appendix III for white paper repositories.
- **Marketing requirement documents (MRDs)**: Typically a company will include some market research or market assessment data in MRDs that are worth looking at.
- **Business plans**: For smaller companies, a business plan will often explore the marketplace and

the need, information that can be helpful for the white paper.

- **Press releases**: Press releases often contain quotes from experts that might be useful for the paper.
- **External press about the company**: When you read what others are saying about the company or product, you may find some valuable information. Be sure to examine blogs as well. For an excellent search of blog content, see search.blogger.com.
- **Industry articles**: Topical articles often include research and marketplace information.
- **Brochures**: Company or product brochures might be helpful to understand how to describe the solution.
- **Key pages from the company website**: Ask about which pages on the company website you should examine. For a big company, it may be hard to know where to look for what matters.
- **Sites that aggregate articles**: A number of article aggregation websites exist that permanently store articles from many sources, helping you speed the research process. A few worth examining include www.findarticles.com and www.keepmedia.com.
- **Datasheets**: For features and benefits of a product or service, datasheets are excellent sources.

This chapter examined the many advantages of using Google for research. It also revealed other important places to look for information that will enhance your white paper. With content from interviews and research in hand, you are ready to begin writing. The next chapter examines the critical process of writing the first page.

✳ Chapter 6 ✳

Writing the First Page

"The two most engaging powers of an author are to make new things familiar and familiar things new."

—Samuel Johnson

The first page of your white paper is the first bite of a big meal. If the taste is right, your reader will sit down at the table and enjoy the entire document. The hardest part of any white paper project is penning the first page. An overwhelming thought of "where to begin" often permeates my mind. At this point—the moment the page is blank—we writers must write something important.

This is extra critical in today's era because your paper is adrift in a sea of information vying for your readers' attention. Combine this with the microsecond attention spans of many readers and you have a real challenge.

How do you rapidly reveal enough information to persuade someone to read your white paper? This chapter will discuss the importance of the first words of your white paper, identify some strategies to draw in your ideal readers, discuss ways to get down to writing and analyze the use of abstracts.

LESSONS FROM IKEA

I clearly remember the first time I wandered into an IKEA megastore. A line from that famous Eagles song came to mind, "Welcome to the Hotel California... You can check out any time you like, but you can never leave."

IKEA, a Swedish-based retail chain that specializes in low-cost household items, designs its stores with only one way in and one way out. The path to freedom mazes shoppers through the entire store. No shortcuts, no easy way to find what you like, only a mile-long zigzagging path from beginning to end, past everything the store has to offer. By the time you reach the checkout line, you've been exposed to far more than you bargained for and you are exhausted.

Sound like some papers you have read or even written? Trudging through heavy or irrelevant content is a curse for most readers.

Carrying the retail analogy a bit further, you can gain some insights from your favorite grocery store. Rather than wandering up and down aisles looking for cough syrup or cayenne pepper, most grocery stores place clerks or helpful signs around the store to guide you. Similarly, a good white paper must guide its readers.

The key to avoiding the IKEA trap is to clearly identify the salient points of the paper in an efficient manner. Avoid making the reader eye more than a few paragraphs before you introduce the objective. Some people use executive summaries, but I prefer to simply state the goal of the piece in the opening paragraphs. Make sure that EVERYTHING you discuss is relevant and related to the topic of the paper.

THE FIRST PAGE FORMULA

Many writers indicate the first page is extremely difficult to write. The fact is, getting started is hard enough and the first page is particularly challenging because of its importance to any white paper.

I studied public speaking in college and one of the key points my professors kept driving home was the concept of an attention-getter. In speech, this is often an alarming fact or something humorous at the onset of the presentation. When it comes to writing white papers, it is equally important to get the attention of the reader.

However, unlike a public speaking engagement, where the audience has an idea what they are about to hear, a white paper must quickly introduce its key points before any startling facts can serve a meaningful purpose.

The following formula will help you gain the attention of your readers. This simple four-step process will aid you in the production of an easy-to-read and persuasive first page. The formula is based on a building process that starts with simple ideas and is carefully expanded until you have your first page.

These are the elements of the first page formula:

1. Identify the reader
2. Summarize the challenge
3. Summarize the solution
4. State the goal

When writing your first page, think of a movie trailer. Popular movies are often summarized in a 30-second clip that persuades people to go see the feature film. They include enough information to entice someone to act; namely to go to the theater. However, good trailers do not give away the full plot of the movie. Similarly, a white paper's first page must provide enough information without giving away the whole story.

The four steps of the first page formula are very important and serve distinct purposes. Revealing the ideal reader quickly filters the audience by describing who will benefit from the white paper. Explaining key challenges builds affinity with readers by highlighting issues they care about and also further filters out those readers who

are not facing similar challenges. Providing a brief introduction to the solution helps readers know what to look
forward to in the white paper. Clearly stating the goal
helps readers understand what they will learn by reading
the white paper.

Begin by roughing out some ideas. Don't worry about
the language. Simply get your ideas into written form,
even if they sound horrible.

Consider the following example for new plastic surgery
equipment:

1. **The ideal reader**: Plastic surgeons
2. **The challenge**: Doctors need to wait for equip-
    ment to be cleaned before they can begin a
    procedure
3. **The solution**: Sterile, disposable equipment
4. **The goal**: To educate doctors on the advantages
    of disposable equipment

Taking these four elements, a working opening can
be easily developed. Here is an option: "Plastic surgeons
performing liposuction must to wait for equipment to
be cleaned, sterilized and cooled before they can start
their next procedure, limiting the number of procedures
performed in a day. New disposable equipment eliminates
this problem by providing doctors sterile tools that are
immediately available and can be discarded after each
procedure. This white paper will explore the advantages
of disposable equipment for plastic surgeons."

Notice that the above opening has a bit more detail
than the initial four elements. The core elements of the
first page formula are simply extemporaneous notes
meant to jog your memory and help you focus your
writing. The plastic surgery example can be easily developed into a few paragraphs by further discussing some
of the challenges faced by the ideal reader. By following
the first page formula, an idea can be expanded into the
opening paragraphs of your white paper.

WHAT TO AVOID ON THE FIRST PAGE

Because the first page is critical to inviting the reader into your document, some topics and styles should be avoided. Steer clear of the following:

Detailed explanations of the solution: Starting the paper with a long-winded explanation of your product, service or solution is to be strictly avoided. These details belong in manuals or brochures, not in white papers. Why? This assumes the reader is specifically interested in finding out more details about your solution. The fact is that most folks are not even sure what they need when they read white papers. Rather, they read them primarily to learn, not to be sold to.

A discussion of features: Product features belong nowhere on the opening page of your white paper. Features only matter once someone has decided to seriously consider your solution. It is always wiser to discuss benefits in the introduction rather than features.

An introduction to your company: Do not introduce the company behind the solution until much later in a white paper. The exception might be a white paper about a very technical product or feature. However, even in these cases, the company providing the solution must be only mentioned lightly. Why? The goal of the opening page of a white paper should be to build affinity with the reader, rather than sell the company.

Describing how the solution works: The process behind the solution can only be adequately addressed once the need has been established. Technical white papers often focus heavily on the "how," but this should only be briefly addressed on the opening page.

Humor: Do not try to open with a long joke. It gets in the way of the core message of the white paper. White papers tend to be much more "to the point" documents. Remember the short attention span of your readers.

PREPARATION FOR WRITING

Sitting down to write can be challenging. I learned early on that I had zones in my day when I could write best. When I was in the zone, I would literally write pages and pages of content. However, when I was outside the zone, I was lucky to get a single page written.

For me, the zone is between 9 AM and 11 AM and from 9 PM to 10 PM. You may find your zone is longer or shorter. However, you will notice that at certain times of the day you are very productive.

During these times, try to clear your schedule and make sure nothing can distract you. In my case, this is particularly difficult because I make it into the office at about 9 AM and my first inclination is to check voicemails, read my e-mail, place some calls and check a few things off my "to do" list. Only by exercising extreme discipline am I able to force myself to do nothing but write during those hours.

So how do you rid yourself of distractions? Here are a few ideas:

- Put your desk phone on "do not disturb" or unplug it
- Turn off your mobile phone
- Do not start up your e-mail
- Shut down your instant messaging application
- Close the door to your office
- Take your shoes off
- Put on some background music or turn on a fan for ambient noise
- Pray for no interruptions and clarity in your writing
- Get a little caffeine in your system

I also let all of my clients know that I am not available for calls or meetings in the morning because it is my writing time. Nearly all of them respect this and they have come to know not to contact me during this time.

Another important tip is to just write and worry about how it sounds later. Some writers like to dictate into tape recorders and others like to just start typing and get all of their thoughts onto a page. I like to take a clipboard, head for a quiet place and just start writing. When I transcribe my notes into Microsoft Word, I tend to iron out some of the writing a bit. Much later, I will review my writing with a critical eye and further refine it.

Another key is to break your project into smaller, manageable sections. For example, rather than making your goal to sit and write an entire white paper, try simply writing the first page. Consider rewarding yourself if you meet your self-imposed deadlines with something nice, like a 30-minute break or a trip to Starbucks.

Some advocate writing the first page last. Their rationale is that by the time most of the paper is complete, you will have everything you need to write a great first page. Although a good idea, I prefer getting the first page down right away. Why? Having the first page complete sets the tone for the entire document and serves as a guidepost to turn back to when you are confused or lose your way.

Before you begin writing, consider some of these tips. Be sure you have read all available supporting material. This will help bring everything important to your mind. Refer to your original outline to familiarize yourself with the key issues. This helps keep you grounded in the goals of the project. Review your interview notes. Those interviews are your best source of content, so be sure to study them before you write.

Getting Words to Paper

Why are white papers so hard to write? Simply put, they require effort. Effort makes us sweat. So what's the trick to getting words to paper? I'd like to think a big part of the problem is having the wrong equipment. You don't send a man into the bush with a butter knife—you have him wield a machete! So what are the tools critical to get underway on white papers?

- **Classical music**: Start by soothing the mind with some tunes that let you focus.
- **Caffeinated beverage**: A little caffeine goes a long way for me.
- **Time**: Don't rush a masterpiece; take some time to think it through.
- **A clipboard**: It's useful to get in the car and go somewhere strange and start writing (or just roll down the window and act like you are going somewhere). A clipboard is your portable table.
- **Dictation software**: Software that translates your recorded voice into editable text is a must-have for two-finger typists.

ABSTRACTS

Abstracts, also known as *executive summaries*, are designed to provide an overview of the critical elements of a white paper. According to an extensive survey of writers, more than 80 percent regularly use abstracts in their white papers.[1]

The abstract typically stands in front of the core content of a white paper, after a title page and before

---

[1] Stelzner, M. (November 2005). *WhitePaperSource.* 2005 White paper writer industry survey: Identifying trends and issues faced by white paper writers, http://www.whitepapersource.com/report/.

the body of the paper. It tends to include the key points about the white paper and occupy its own page.

Abstracts are good for very technical white papers, long reports and websites that encourage a white paper download—akin to a sales pitch for the paper. Many writers argue that NOT using an abstract within the white paper is arrogant because readers do not have time to read white papers in their entirety.

However, there are many valid reasons to forgo the abstract. Let's begin by examining where abstracts are NOT used:

- Magazine and trade publication articles
- Brochures
- Case studies
- Datasheets
- Direct mail
- Advertising

Among the typical tools used for sales and marketing efforts, abstracts are clearly absent. If the white paper is a marketing tool, adding an abstract should be reconsidered.

It is wise to let readers know—up front—what they will learn from your paper. However, the abstract is not always the best vehicle to achieve this end.

Consider the primary goal of your white paper. For many, the objective is to educate and ultimately persuade readers. When the goal is to persuade, it does not help to give away the big "Ah-hah!" right off the bat. This means do not include the jewels of your paper in an abstract. Rather, provide enough early information to encourage the reader to go further into the white paper.

A very persuasive and compelling white paper will grab readers and suck them in, like a good novel. If you put an abstract or executive summary at the start of your paper, people may read the abstract, but will they actually read the paper? The power is in the paper, NOT in the abstract.

It is true that your readers are very busy and you need to get to the point quickly. It is also true that most readers are skimmers and do not necessarily intend to read the entire white paper. So, borrow from the masters. Get your foot in the door and open it slowly, providing valuable content as the reader begins to walk through your paper. Lead with the key points in the opening paragraphs. If you take the problem-solution approach, discuss the top challenges and include a brief teaser on the solution in the first two paragraphs.

By integrating the key elements of an abstract into the opening paragraphs of your white paper, you inform your readers and encourage them to go deeper into your white paper.

This chapter revealed a proven approach to writing the first few paragraphs of your white paper, examined how to get down to the act of writing and analyzed the use of abstracts. A key part of the white paper's first page is the title. The next chapter will take an in-depth look at the art of crafting titles and subtitles.

✳ Chapter 7 ✳

The Compelling Title

W hat's the value of a title? A title is a nice suit, a cocktail dress, a pretty face, a head-turner or any other metaphor that grabs your attention. The title is your white paper's absolute first impression. In it rests success or failure for the words that lie beyond, waiting for a reader. If the title does not encourage someone to read further, the ink that coats your white paper will never be discovered.

This chapter will help you add life to your white paper title, in turn bringing readers through the door and ensuring they actually start down the road to reading your masterpiece.

TITLES MAKE OR BREAK WHITE PAPERS

Relevant titles provide insight into your subject and capture the attention of your ideal readers. Everyone is busy and relevance matters. When searching the Internet, you most likely type in a few keywords and scan a list of results, looking for relevance. What compels you to click on some listings rather than others? Why don't you visit every website that comes up on your screen? The mental filtering process provides insight into why we decide to read some things and pass on others. It also illustrates the importance of the title.

Marketing professionals refer to the "3-30-3 rule" when creating content that attracts readers. The rule states that you only have 3 seconds to hook any reader. That means you need a great title and subtitle to capture readers. If you tickle the interest of readers in the first 3 seconds, they will allocate another 30 seconds to read further. If your message is very relevant and interesting, the reader will spend 3 more minutes with your white paper. Your goal is get readers into the 30-second zone, and the ONLY way to do that is to write an excellent title.

Malcolm Gladwell, author of the bestseller *Blink: The Power of Thinking Without Thinking,* adds credence to this theory with his discussion of thin slicing.[1] Based on existing "brain-science," Gladwell explains that in this age of information overload, people make snap decisions based on thin slices of information and time. He describes our unconscious as a giant supercomputer that allows us to immediately determine the importance of experiences.

Peter Bowerman, author of *The Well-Fed Writer*, states, "The goal of writing anything is to have it be read. A little elementary? Perhaps, but judging by the lame titles people create, maybe it isn't so elementary. A title is a lure. It's the hook of any article, book or white paper. A good one will draw a reader in; a weak one will have that reader turn the page, move on to the next shelf and click the next link."

John Moore, a marketing guru responsible for creating the branding for Whole Foods Market and Starbucks Coffee, says, "Capturing the attention of people is becoming much more difficult. This attention challenge pertains to white paper titles as much as it does to advertising."

---

[1] Gladwell, M. (2005). *Blink: The power of thinking without thinking.* New York: Little, Brown and Company.

Robert W. Bly, author of numerous books on the art of writing, simply states, "A well-written title creates a desire to obtain and read the white paper." In Bly's book, *The White Paper Marketing Handbook*, he explains, "Whether prospects eagerly send for your white paper or pass it by is determined largely by the title."[2]

The title becomes even more important if your white paper will be posted in an online resource center, library or white paper directory, because the paper will be competing for attention along with tens, hundreds or thousands of other documents.

IMPORTANT TITLE CRAFTING TIPS

When thinking about titles, it is very important to revisit your needs assessment (see Chapter 2) and examine the objective of your white paper. If the goal is to generate leads or even help close a sale, the title will be critical. If your white paper is a very technical document, it is still wise to come up with a refined title.

Bowerman's most persuasive tip for writing titles involves **making the title a promise**, or a result the reader will achieve after reading the white paper. He explains, "This 'promise' idea harkens back to the old features and benefits discussion. A promise is a benefit, meaning it's all about the readers and what's important to them. It tells them why they should read the book, article or white paper. *The Well-Fed Writer* is a benefits-oriented title, and as such, definitely speaks to that reader. If I'd called it *A Guide to Freelance Writing*, in addition to being exquisitely dull, it would have been a features-oriented title, meaning it was all about the book itself and not about the reader. Not every project lends itself to the promise idea, but the more you can keep your title audience-focused and benefits-focused, the better off you'll be."

---

[2] Bly, R. (2006). *The white paper marketing handbook*. Mason, Ohio: Thomson Higher Education.

Bowerman adds that the title should help readers immediately understand what your white paper is about, it should be clever and effective, and you should consider performing a sanity-check of your title with a number of people.

Alternatively, Bly says that writers should **hook into a dominant resonant emotion** of readers. He explains that appealing to emotion is just as important as intellect and provides the following example of a successful ad he drafted: "Important news for every IT professional who has ever felt like telling an end user, 'Go to hell!'" In his book, *The White Paper Marketing Handbook*, Bly also references the **3 U's formula** for crafting titles. It states that a good title should be ultra-specific, unique and useful to your ideal readers.

Moore adds that titles should **respect the readers' intellect**, "For example, mid-level marketers at *Fortune 500* companies will immediately know what the acronyms CPM and CRM stand for. There is no need to write Cost Per Thousand or Customer Relationship Management in the title." Moore also mentioned that titles can introduce new terms that are self-explanatory. For example, marketing professionals may not understand the term "conversational capital," but might be intrigued by a title such as, "Building Strong Brands Using Conversational Capital."

MarketingSherpa.com, a web portal for marketing professionals, examined white paper titling with Internet publisher CNET.com, the owner of one of the largest online repositories of white papers, ITPapers.com.[3] Because CNET has more than 25,000 white papers posted on its network, examining how its users responded to white paper titles can reveal much.

An important finding was the **use of keywords in the title** of a white paper. For example, white papers with the term "spyware" in the title were 77 percent more likely

---

[3] MarketingSherpa. (October 6, 2005). New research data: How to title your white papers to generate more downloads from best prospects, http://library.marketingsherpa.com/barrier.cfm?CID=3090.

to be read than those with the term "anti-spyware." The lesson here is to stick with words that will resonate with the ideal reader.

One valuable way to see which terms have greater market acceptance is to do a Google search on your possible keywords. The more they occur, the more likely they are the accepted standard. For example, at the time of this writing, the term "anti-spyware" occurred three times more frequently than the term "antispyware" (no hyphen).

Shorter titles outperform longer ones. The most downloaded papers had 20 percent fewer words than the least downloaded white papers. For example, among papers on digital security, the most viewed paper was titled, "The Starter PKI Program," and the least popular paper was titled, "An Introduction to Enterprise Public Key Infrastructure (PKI)." Both papers addressed the same topic, but the one with the shorter title outperformed the wordier one. The human eye's ability to quickly scan shorter titles may explain their increased readership.

Some other proven tips include:

Use a number in the title: Numbers can be very alluring in titles and are used heavily in the world of article writing. By mentioning "10 reasons to upgrade" or "6 mistakes every writer should avoid," you convey to your reader that your paper includes tangible, rapidly digestible facts.

Include a lively and active verb: Action words imply a benefit that can be achieved with the white paper. Words such as "eliminating," "growing," "speeding" and "enhancing," engage readers by implying achievable results. By telling readers what's in it for them, you lure them in.

Address the why: Does your title explain why readers should read your white paper? It should. For example, "How to Write a White Paper," is more compelling than "The Art of White Paper Writing" because it implies the reader will learn how to write a white paper. Sometimes the why is accomplished in the subtitle and other times in the title.

Use a colon: Often subtitles are excluded from the descriptive title of a white paper when they are listed online. One way to ensure subtitles are listed as part of the title is by using a colon. When you use a colon, you can lead with a single word or a catchy phrase and immediately follow through with a description of the topic. For example, "Multimodality: The Next Wave of Mobile Phone Interaction."

Job titles: If you are targeting a very specific audience, it might be wise to include the title of the ideal reader or the title of the type of person who would most benefit from your topic in the white paper title. For example, "Improving Knowledge Worker Performance with Push Technology" or "The Most Important Question Every HR Professional Should Ask New Hires."

Write the title late in the process: Try drafting the title after you have made significant progress on your white paper. Once you have hashed out the key problems and benefits of your solution, a good title might emerge naturally.

The following list includes less-than-desirable titles and improved alternatives:

Poor Title	Better Title
Enterprise Business Intelligence: Strategies and Technologies for Deploying BI on an Enterprise Scale	Business Intelligence: An Intelligent Move or Not?
Addressing Regulatory Compliance Issues	Simple Steps to Compliance: How Advanced Tools Assure Regulatory Conformance
Bluetooth White Paper	Cutting the Cord: The Benefits of Bluetooth Wireless
Disaster Recovery: Best Practices White Paper	Are You Prepared for Disaster? 10 Steps That Could Save Your Business
Web Application Vulnerabilities and Security	Securing Your Enterprise: 10 Things You Need to Know Now

TESTING TITLES

Once you think you have a few winning titles, it is important to test them and see if they resonate with readers. The testing process will almost always result in a better title for your white paper. Consider how the title for this book came to be. After significant thought and brainstorming, I finalized this book title down to three options:

- The Well-Written White Paper: A Complete Guide to the Art of Writing White Papers
- Crafting the "Must-Read" White Paper: A Complete Guide to the Art of Writing White Papers
- Writing White Papers: The Complete Guide to the Art of White Paper Writing

The third option was the bland original title I had come up with early in the process of writing this book. I had previously eliminated it, but I decided to see how it performed. The first title was my personal favorite prior to my testing.

More than 70 people voted for their favorite titles and the results were very shocking. Among my 40 or so friends, they generally preferred the first title, "The Well-Written White Paper." However, among 30 professional writers—my ideal readers—they overwhelmingly preferred the third title, "Writing White Papers."

On further examination, I determined that my inner circle of friends did not understand the topic and were more marketing folks than writers. During this process, one writer suggested I make a more compelling subtitle. I ultimately ended up with "Writing White Papers: How to Capture Readers and Keep Them Engaged." I carefully calculated that leading with a short, descriptive title and following through with a more compelling subtitle would attract the largest group of potential readers to this book. I further tested the title and it turned out to be well-received by friends and professionals.

Had I never conducted a survey, I would have ended up with a much less compelling title. Be sure you test the titles of your critical white papers. The power of feedback from large groups of people, particularly among your ideal readers, is very useful.

Google Testing

Another way to test titles is to perform an A|B split test with Google's inexpensive pay-per-click advertising system. Because white papers perform very well as responses to online advertisements, running ads for your white paper will provide excellent feedback.

Google AdWords allows you to setup multiple small text ads. Each ad can have a custom headline and body text, and can link to a unique location. If you are torn between two or more possible titles, you might consider creating multiple versions of your white paper ad, each with a different title. Each ad can link directly to the appropriate version of your white paper. Alternatively, you can simply create all the ads with different titles and have them link to a single version of your white paper.

Google will show you which ads had the highest click-through rates, providing immediate feedback on the performance of one title over the next. You only need to run ads for a week to determine which one generates the highest clicks. Once you have a clear winner, you can try slightly altering your title to see if the click-through rates significantly change.

SUBTITLES

If a title is the bait, then the subtitle is the hook and line that will draw the reader into your document. "If a good title captures a reader's attention, then an appropriate subtitle will captivate readers and cause them to spend a few extra moments with the paper," states Moore. Back to the 3-30-3 rule, remember that your readers will only allocate a few seconds when deciding whether to read your white paper. The title alone will occupy just a portion of those 3 seconds. The subtitle helps clarify to readers exactly what your white paper is all about.

Subtitles have many advantages. Bly explains one: "A straightforward, descriptive subtitle allows you to use a title that may be dramatic, but not as clear or descriptive." When you use a descriptive subtitle, you can get more creative with your title. For example, "Forever Lost: Why Employees Steal Company Property" enables the use of a simple and attention-getting title.

Bowerman states, "Subtitles reinforce, clarify and elaborate on the title, filling in more blanks for the reader." For example, "Curtailing the Piracy Epidemic: A Case for Hardware Security Keys" accomplishes two objectives. First, it addresses businesses that are losing money due to software piracy and second, it addresses the solution in the subtitle.

WHAT TO AVOID

Below are a few things to avoid when crafting your title and subtitle:

Do not be cute: Humor has a limited place in white paper titles. Research shows that clever word plays do not draw as many readers as focused and succinct titles.

Never mention company or product names: Remember that a white paper is not a brochure or product datasheet. By using the title, "The RenCompSys Auditory Enhancement Product," you are announcing your white paper is a sales document.

Do not make it feature-oriented: People only care about features after they are convinced you can solve their problems. Rather than, "The Value of 100X CD Writing," consider translating the feature into a benefit, such as "Meeting Backup Windows: The Case for Next-Generation Optical Storage."

Do not use terms the reader will not understand: Keep your ideal readers in mind. If you use terms that are not self-explanatory or go over the heads of your readers, you will never engage them. If you are writing to upper management about challenges faced in the IT department, avoid using buzzwords or technical terms that only an engineer would relate to.

Avoid wordy and long titles: Moore explains, "Wordy titles may also turn away readers who will assume if the author can't keep the title succinct, then the white paper will also be wayward and too lengthy."

A compelling title brings readers into your document, but excellent content is what compels them to stay with your white paper to the end. The next chapter provides guidance for developing core white paper content that will engage your readers.

✳ Chapter 8 ✳

Writing the Core

*"'Think simple' as my old master used to say—
meaning reduce the whole of its parts into the simplest
terms."*

—Frank Lloyd Wright, architect.[1]

W right was right, the easiest way to conquer a
complex project is to break it down into easily
accomplished tasks. As you write each small
section of your white paper, you ascend the stairs of
progress toward completion. This chapter will equip you
to make the journey.

Now that you have established an outline (see Chapter
3) and formulated your first page (see Chapter 6), it's
time to get down to core of your white paper. Imagine a
new house with the architectural plans and framing in
place. You can visualize how your home will look, but you
still need to put up the drywall, add the electricity, paint
the walls, carpet the floors and furnish the rooms. There
is much to do, but no single task is overly complex.

---

[1] Fitzhenry, R. I. (1987). *Barnes & Noble book of quotations.* New York:
HarperCollins.

This chapter will provide you a playbook with proven strategies that will help you create the core aspects of your white paper. The words between the first and last pages of your white paper represent the bulk of your work. For that reason, this chapter is the largest in this book. It will address everything from developing a market drivers discussion to writing a compelling call to action at the end of your document.

MARKET DRIVERS

The hammer drives the nail. The traffic officer diverts traffic. A sunny day gets me driving to the beach. What drives your readers to need your solution? What are the key market movements and industry trends that justify the need for change?

The word "drivers," at its core, implies change agents: What is the impetus that is pointing people in a certain direction? This section of your white paper should show your readers that something is emerging in the marketplace that demands their attention.

Why Market Drivers Matter

White papers are generally persuasive documents; thus, it is important to provide proof that your marketplace is changing. For example, if you are writing a white paper about document management, a market drivers section might discuss research that demonstrates businesses have increasingly been bogged down by physical paperwork.

By laying out trends early in the white paper, readers might be convinced they are behind the times and read on further. When you quote trusted third-party sources, market drivers add credibility to your white paper.

Sample Market Drivers Section

The ability to communicate is one of the most mission-critical requirements for any organization. For decades, the phone has been an essential business tool that has connected people across the office, across town, across the nation and around the globe.

Despite its ubiquitous nature, the essence of the business telephone has remained the same, while other communications technologies, such as mobile phones and the Internet, have dramatically evolved. With the exception of a few features, such as caller-ID and voicemail, the phone has not changed much—until recently. IT managers now face the inevitable convergence of voice and data.

Businesses are rapidly adopting IP telephony solutions. For example, in 2004, sales of IP telephony solutions outpaced conventional PBXs for the first time, and Gartner predicts that 90 percent of new system sales will be IP-based by 2010.[2] Furthermore, sales of IP telephony systems grew 36 percent between 2004 and 2005 alone, according to Infonetics Research.[3] By the end of 2007, IP telephony will be deployed by 45 percent of U.S. businesses, predicts Osterman Research.[4]

---

[2] Morrissey, P. (March 17, 2005). *Network computing*. VoIP: Join the party, http://www.networkcomputing.com/showitem.jhtml?docid=1605f1.
[3] Rash, W. (June 6, 2005). *eWeek*. PBX sales drop hides IP success story, http://www.eweek.com/article2/0,1895,1824920,00.asp.
[4] McGann, R. (February 23, 2005). *ClickZ.com*. VoIP poised to take flight? http://www.clickz.com/stats/sectors/software/article.php/3485231.

The Components of Market Drivers

The market drivers section usually follows the opening paragraphs of your white paper and provides a great way to boost your credibility and persuade the reader that the claims you are making are true. Remember that market drivers are about your industry and not about your solution (a related, but important distinction), so be sure not to talk about the sales of your particular product.

Here are a few things you can do when writing the market drivers section. First, you should write objectively. It is important to speak clearly and not appear too biased. If you are making claims that are clearly exaggerated, your reader will question your validity.

Second, you should quote reputable third-party sources when making statements that involve numbers of any kind. For example, if you state, "Corporate workers spend an average of two hours per day performing personal tasks on their computers, costing corporations billions of dollars in lost revenues," you had better present some hard evidence to back up your claim. Even though it may be true, in the absence of a good source you would be better off saying something like, "Personal Internet usage is stealing away excessive amounts of workforce labor time."

Market drivers are typically comprised of two underlying strategies, third-party evidence and logical arguments.

Third-party evidence

Ideally, you want to use as much third-party evidence as possible because it adds trustworthiness to your white paper. This type of information comes in the form of a statistic or quote from an expert (see Sample Market Drivers section).

Trade magazine articles related to your topic are one of the first places to look for third-party evidence. These articles often contain useful statistics from major industry analysts or actual interviews with key people that can be referenced in your white paper. Some other places to find third-party evidence include press releases from your competitors, Internet research (see Chapter 5) and in existing PowerPoint presentations.

Ideally, you should reference recognized names when actually quoting people. You could even pick up the phone, speak to experts and then quote them in the market drivers portion of your white paper.

However, simply quoting someone for the sake of having a quotation in this section of your white paper is ill-advised. If the person being quoted does not have credibility, it may turn off your readers and they may stop reading the rest of your white paper. Remember that your goal is to get readers to the end of your document so they can act in the way you want them to (such as make a call or place an order).

For example, if you are writing about changes in network technology, it would be much better to quote an analyst than an executive working for the sponsoring company. As a matter of course, keep all employees of the company completely out of the white paper to avoid the perception your paper is biased or a hard-sell document. Also, keep references to the company's customers out of this section of the white paper.

When you come across excellent research, you may not have a very good citation to reference. This is particularly common when you find a juicy nugget in a PowerPoint presentation. Often, these presentations will have no citations or will simply say something like "Forrester Research." The problem is that white papers need to be much more specific when citing an expert or source. You might need to track down the author of the presentation and find out where that citation came from. Because a white paper is a formal published work, you should footnote all citations using recognized standards (see Appendix III).

Logical arguments

If your topic is so narrow (or so broad) that no one has discussed it prior to your paper, you will need to rely exclusively on logical arguments in the market driver section. Alternatively, you can combine logical arguments and very broad third-party evidence that hints at a change in your market.

Logical arguments are claims based on commonly understood information. Here are some sample logical arguments:

- Overworked employees are generally more stressed
- New regulatory legislation generates previously unforeseen costs for businesses
- As baby boomers age, the need for more senior housing will likely increase

These logical arguments are generally not challenged because they appeal to information that is well-understood by your readers. However, even though the reader understands this information, do not assume it should be overlooked in the market drivers section. When you do appeal to these commonly held understandings, you are building affinity with your readership and are strengthening your case.

An additional note, when making logical arguments, it is wise to use words such as "generally," "typically," "likely" and "usually." This helps protect your white paper from making absolute claims that could turn off your readers.

Now that you understand how to write the market drivers section of your white paper, a great transition is the problem development.

PROBLEM DEVELOPMENT

"Houston, we have a problem," were the words spoken by Tom Hanks as he portrayed Astronaut Jim Lovell on the Apollo 13 mission. Why has this line become so ingrained in our culture? The answer: Because problems get our attention. Similarly, leading with problems or needs early in your white paper is a very powerful method to gain the interest of your readers.

Describing problems that occur when your solution is "not in place," helps educate and build affinity with your readers. The key to this section of your white paper is to focus on the need or challenge that emerges when your solution is absent.

Think about it this way: If your white paper is about the introduction of a new form of high-definition television, you might want to focus on the challenges or limitations faced by the existing standard. These issues may or may not be known by your reader, but placing them early in the document will help build a persuasive case that your solution is best for your reader's needs.

Why Problems Matter

By discussing problems and the implications of not dealing with them, you set up an opportunity to reaffirm the reader's concerns and reveal new issues that may not have been considered.

Concentrating on your readers and their pain points is an excellent way to draw them into your white paper. Why? First, people do not like to be sold to. Discussing challenges helps your white paper appear to be something useful to your reader. Secondly, if the reader can relate to the issues you identify in this section of your white paper, you are sending the message "these guys understand what I am going through." The result is often greater credibility.

Talking about problems and their roots is a form of educational marketing. It reveals issues your readers may not have realized were caused by the absence of your solution. In his book on marketing with white papers, Robert W. Bly explains why this is important: "Marketers who educate their customers build better relationships with their marketplace and project a positive, leadership-oriented image. They are seen as more honest and credible than marketers whose only objective seems to be to sell their product rather than solve the customer's problem."[5] Bly is correct that the attempt to solve some-one's problems—a process he calls *edu-marketing*—adds more credibility to a white paper.

Including a problem discussion has numerous advantages to any white paper. When you discuss problems, you:

- Demonstrate your understanding of the challenges faced by your ideal reader
- Build affinity by clearly articulating challenges that the reader shares
- Filter out unqualified prospects by discussing issues these readers cannot relate to
- Establish greater credibility by introducing objective reasons problems exist
- Reveal issues your reader may have never considered

The problem statement borrows heavily from the traditional advertising world. Often, print, radio and television advertisements will lead with challenges faced by their target audience. Here are few examples:

- **"It's your bright idea. Keep it safe."** This problem statement came from an ad for Maxtor hard drives. The implied message is: If you don't backup your data, it isn't safe.
- **"You didn't open a business to work for us."** This line was in an ad for DHL delivery services. The implied message is: Working hard to ship packages is not why you are in business.
- **"Feel like a small fish in a big pond? Switch to TD Waterhouse."** This came from a brokerage services ad and the implied message is: You are not getting the attention you deserve.

---

[5] Bly, R. W. (2006). *The white paper marketing handbook.* Mason, Ohio: Thomson Higher Education.

- **"What does zeroing-out your credit cards feel like?"** This question is from an Ameriquest Mortgage ad. The implied message is: Your high credit card balances are stressing you out.

It is important to note that even though problem development is a major strategy in many traditional advertisements, white papers are to ads what books are to book covers. Ads reduce issues to the fewest possible words, while white papers develop them in detail. However, ads are much more prevalent than white papers and we can learn from their common problem-based approach.

Sample Problem Development
Retaining Volunteers: Government affairs organizations walk a fine line between inundating volunteers with action requests and not properly utilizing the strength of their grassroots supporters. Make too many requests and lose the volunteers, make too few and eliminate the feeling of ownership. The trick to retaining volunteers is to make it easy for them to learn about the issues important to them and act when needed. Many organizations write letters and make calls to volunteers. This time-consuming and costly process does not make it easy for volunteers to take action. Ideally, volunteers' areas of interest are recorded and communications are targeted only to relevant volunteers. In addition, modern technology enables automated identification of who has or has not acted on targeted communications.

The Components of Problem Development

Discussing key challenges or needs faced by your ideal readers should be done early in the white paper, often following a market drivers section or the first page. When discussing problems, it is very important to keep them in context of your ideal reader (see Chapter 2). If you developed a comprehensive outline (see Chapter 3), the problems section of your outline should provide a list of the top challenges you will be discussing in this portion of your paper.

There may be many different challenges that can be addressed, but they must be salient to the ideal reader. When developing problems, always ask yourself, "Can the ideal reader relate to these problems and are they relevant?"

When you have a short list of problems (between three and six), try to determine what they all have in common. This familiar thread will help establish the high-level problem statement. This core overarching challenge should be condensed into to a single sentence. Be sure all the problems are compelling and appropriate to your primary target audience.

Everyone reading this book should relate to writer's block, so let's develop a problem around the concept. I will start by identifying my ideal reader as a writer who is tasked with many additional "non-writing" responsibilities.

Think about this question. What are some of the challenges that occur when you try to sit down and write—especially when you are under a deadline? Jot them down in your mind. A few might include distractions from e-mail and the phone ringing, pure exhaustion because there is too much going on and finally, the desire to make your words sound perfect before proceeding to the next sentence. These may not be the same as your list, but let's work with them.

The next step is to determine the common thread that all the problems share. One approach might be the inability to write more than a few paragraphs in a single sitting. This could be developed into a high-level problem such as, "Writers often find it difficult to quickly produce significant amounts of content in a single sitting" or,

"Writing sizeable blocks of copy in a single session is nearly impossible."

From this newly developed high-level challenge, you can begin writing your problem section and its key implications or problem statements. The implications or related problems might be further developed from the initial list to something such as: (1) "Writing assignments are rarely completed on schedule," (2) "Articulating key ideas is difficult" and (3) "The opportunity for taking on additional writing assignments is reduced." With this data, you can begin putting meat onto the bones of your white paper.

Problems can be developed from a number of different approaches. When brainstorming them, look at the list below to spur some ideas.

People problems: Issues that affect individuals or groups of people are a powerful focus area for some white papers. These types of problems might examine employees, customers, suppliers, partners and so on. You can concentrate on the individual human toll, such as employees who cannot get their jobs done quickly because they cannot find what they need. Alternatively, you can examine problems that impact groups of people. For example, when the rumors of layoffs spread through the office, worker morale declines.

Process problems: Process problems are issues that emerge from poor practices. Unlike people problems, process challenges are focused on the way a function is performed. For example, a company that developed a new computer interconnect technology might focus on the slow, inefficient path that data must travel with current technology. The more technical the white paper, the more likely process problems will be used.

Quality problems: Quality problems often focus on the result of poor functions. For example, a manufacturer of liposuction needles for fat reinsertion might talk about how traditional stainless steel needles injure fat cells, forcing physicians to insert excess fat, leading to inconsistent results.

Absent problems: Absent problems are issues that occur when something is not present. These types of problems are typically issues people do not realize they have and are excellent material for white papers that introduce new technology. For example, prior to the existence of cell phones, stranded drivers had no easy way to notify authorities when they needed help.

Once you have clearly defined a list of problems, you are ready to develop them into compelling arguments. Your high-level problem statement should have been introduced in the first page of your white paper (see Chapter 6). Because the problem section is near the beginning of the white paper, you do not need to repeat the high-level problem again in this section of your paper. Instead, you may want to introduce the related problems.

For example, "There are three primary challenges associated with the improper management of documents and business information: lost data, inefficient processes and regulatory noncompliance." The introductory sentence sets the stage for the rest of the problems by simply listing them.

Each of your problems could be broken into its own subsection with a clear headline. The core of each problem can be easily developed by following this simple formula:

1. Make a claim
2. Back up the claim with supporting data
3. Clarify the risks
4. Hint at the solution

Making the claim: Lead with your specific problem statement. Going back to our writer's block example, we could begin with the claim, "Writing assignments are rarely completed on schedule." When making a claim, it is wise to specifically state the problem, clearly and concisely.

Supporting data: After you have put your claim out there, back it up with supporting data, which might include logical arguments or third-party evidence. For example, you might say, "Research from the Acme Writers Survey (fictitious for this example), revealed that 67 percent of writers indicated they rarely submit projects on schedule."

The risks: After you have made a clear case that the problem really exists, talk about the implications of the challenge to your ideal readers. For example, "Writers who are consistently late submitting their work will impact product launches, costing the company lost revenue. Furthermore, employees who cannot complete tasks on schedule are likely to be less valued than those who are consistently on time."

Solution hint: Briefly hint at the solution without mentioning your specific product or service. This shows the reader that there is hope and keeps him or her engaged in your white paper. For example, "Fortunately, new tools are emerging to help writers increase their efficiency."

Avoid Talking Down to Your Audience
Beware of belittling your readers. It is important to understand exactly whom you are targeting. If the reader has a relatively high level of knowledge on the topic you are writing about, it might be wise to avoid elementary discussions in your presentation of the problems and the solution.

Sophisticated readers expect well-developed arguments that speak directly to them. Thus, if you are speaking to an IT director about service-level agreements (something they are very familiar with), do not define what they are or spend too much of your paper introducing the basic challenges that emerge when service-level agreements are not in place. Rather, you might focus on the attributes of a good one verses a poor one, or some other area with which the reader is less familiar.

HISTORICAL OVERVIEW

Musical artist Sting boldly proclaimed, "History will teach us nothing" in the mid-1980s. However, I beg to differ with this melody master. History can be very powerful, especially when used in a white paper. The future is built on the past and sometimes we forget where we came from. By demonstrating how a marketplace has changed, you are educating your readers and have the opportunity to introduce market advancements that serve as powerful introductions to your solution.

Why History Matters

The historical overview section of your white paper serves as an excellent transition between the problem development and the solution introduction. Why? Typically, solutions have evolved over time. If your reader has some preconceived notion of how his or her problems should be addressed, you can easily show how they might be outdated in this section of your paper.

In addition, a brief history overview can also bring a reader quickly up to speed on market advancements. If you are writing a white paper that is attempting to educate readers or establish thought leadership, it is very useful to include this type of an overview.

Some people object to sandwiching a history section between the problem and the solution because the white paper has already primed readers for a solution to their challenges and discussing history next might stop people from continuing with the paper. However, it is important to reassess your ideal readers and determine their level of topical knowledge. If that level of understanding is low, it might make sense to include a historical overview. If you have a mixed readership of very knowledgeable and less-experienced readers, perhaps a few short paragraphs might be in order. However, I generally recommend a historical overview for most white papers.

Here are some of the advantages to developing a discussion on the history of your topic. History discussions provide:

- Information your readers generally find interesting
- Added credibility to your paper
- A link between the problem and how it has been addressed in the past
- An avenue to covertly show how the competition is behind the times
- A useful way to discuss what has led to the modern-day dilemma solved by your solution
- An opportunity to introduce new technology or techniques before you discuss your solution

Sample Historical Overview
Identity Verification: A Historical Perspective
In the 1980s, financial institutions had very basic safeguards that could only verify that Social Security numbers were valid and not issued to deceased persons. In addition, addresses and phone numbers that were involved in previous cases of fraud were flagged as suspicious.

By the 1990s, identities were validated by determining if a person's Social Security number was consistent with his or her birth date. Systems could also match ZIP codes with telephone area codes to determine if an application was valid. By the late 1990s, many aspects of a person's identity could be verified using a third-party database.

In the early 2000s, systems were developed that leveraged customer data integration technology to bring multiple aspects of a person's identity together from many sources. Issues such as changes of

(continued)

address, marriage name changes and divorces could quickly be validated to reduce false-positive rates.

Today, multiple external databases can combine in- and out-of-wallet information to provide a greater level of validation. For example, questions such as "What was your previous address?" can be asked for authentication purposes. Using modern analytic tools, systems can also determine if a Social Security number was mistyped. These advanced solutions intelligently analyze multiple sources of data to accurately predict the likelihood of fraud. The future involves access to new and improved databases to better verify and authenticate customers.

The Components of a Historical Overview

The historical overview section of your white paper is typically comprised of a few major advancements that occurred during a specified period. Determine how far back in time you need to go to make your point. Although it may be interesting to provide an overview of the last few decades, it may be more effective to examine the last few years.

Because there are so many different angles to discuss history, it is useful to reexamine your goals and brainstorm some possible historical topics. For example, if your paper is on water treatment, you could examine its history from many perspectives, such as:

- How was water treated in ancient times?
- What chemicals are no longer used to treat water?
- Who invented the concept of water treatment?
- How has water treatment been performed in the past?
- What recent technological advancements altered the way water is treated?

- How has the need to treat water changed due to social activities, such as urbanization?
- When did bottled water come on the scene?

The above examples provide only a sampling of how history might be discussed in your paper. It is wise to focus on only a few historical topics, rather than every one on your list. Why? The goal of this section of your paper is to first transition your reader toward the solution and secondly to educate.

The Importance of Accuracy

When talking about history, do not rewrite it. Be sure you have your facts in order and you get the details right. There is nothing more embarrassing than accidentally misrepresenting history. However, you are not writing a history book, so you do not need to provide an in-depth discussion on the topic. Nonetheless, you should have the facts in order and your time references should be accurate.

For example, if you are writing about the Internet and you say it first came on the scene in the year 2000, you will look bad. If you say it was popularized in the mid-1990s, you will look good. If you say the United States Department of Defense began a network in the late 1960s that closely resembled the Internet, you will look even more accurate. The point is to discuss history in such a way that it serves your goals and purposes, while remaining accurate.

Discussing Dates

When discussing dates, you may find it difficult to nail down an exact day when something occurred. I often ask my clients for a range of time, or their gut feelings. Consider the topic of e-mail. If you do not know when it became popular you can work backward. You could say any of the following:

- E-mail became a common form of communication by the 1990s.
- Over the last decade, businesses became heavily dependent on e-mail.
- Over the last few years, e-mail has become one of the most common forms of business communication.

You could perform a quick Internet search and find more specific details. For example, in minutes you could search Google or Wikipedia.org and find out that two credible sources put the first e-mail between 1965 and 1971. Alternatively, you could say, "By the early 1970s, the first e-mail was being transmitted between computers."

If you are uncertain about a date or even a range of years, talk in terms of decades. The wider your reference dates, the safer your claims will be. However, the more accurate you can be with dates, the more credible your paper will be.

When discussing history, there is really no need to mention the specific month or day of the month. In a white paper, such superfluous details will only serve to distract your readers. Feel free to cite sources if you think the reader might want to find out more information.

Introducing the Future

The historical overview section is also a great place to talk about where the future of your marketplace is going. For example, if you were writing about mobile phones, you might mention how the future will see the convergence of radio and television into the mobile communication experience. If you do mention the future, make sure your solution somehow ties into that future. Thus, if your solution provides the platform to make such mobile conversion a reality, this serves as an excellent transition.

THE GENERIC SOLUTION

A man was walking through a grocery store parking lot and saw a lady in distress by a broken-down car. She asked him, "Sir, how do I go about fixing my problem?" He answered, "It looks like you need a mechanic who specializes in engine repair." She replied, "Where can I find someone nearby?" He smiled and said, "You're standing next to one on his day off." She responded, "If you are willing to help me, I will gladly pay you for your efforts."

This story is a small demonstration of how to introduce a solution. The man could have said from the outset, "I'm a mechanic and you should hire me to solve your problem," but instead he said the lady needed a mechanic.

By classifying the needed solution into a generic category rather than a specific service or product, a white paper can increase the likelihood readers will not feel like they are being sold to. In the end, this approach is more persuasive than a hard-sell.

Most folks think that talking about their solution is one of the easiest parts of the white paper project until I tell them they generally should not mention their product by name, at least not yet. "What!? How do I talk about my product without mentioning its name and why would that be of any value?", they might protest.

Before addressing that objection, I remind clients that a white paper is NOT a "hard-sell" marketing tool. Rather, it is a persuasive soft-sell resource. In general, people do not like to be sold to, especially on paper. However, as Mary Poppins eloquently sang, "A spoonful of sugar helps the medicine go down." By adding something sweet to your white paper, you increase the likelihood it is fully digested. Introducing a categorical solution rather than a specific one reduces the perception of bias.

Why Generic Solutions Matter

Finding solutions to challenges is the main reason people seek white papers. Most white papers do present solutions. However, many immediately go in for the kill and speak of their particular product or service details.

An alternative approach is to perform an opening act with a generic, high-level solution description. By warming up the reader, you prepare him or her to accept your key solution message with greater persuasive power when it is presented later in the white paper.

Imagine you need to hang a picture on your wall and you have never gone about that task before. Would you seek out a 21-ounce fiberglass hammer with a magnetic nail start and 1 1/4 inch zinc-plated finishing nails, or a hammer and nails? Before you can concentrate on the options, you first need to understand you require a hammer and nails.

Generic solution discussions:

- Reduce reader intimidation
- Define a solution in an easy-to-understand manner
- Begin the persuasive process
- Eliminate the perception that readers are being sold a specific solution
- Allow the sponsoring company to define the solution in an advantageous manner
- Can redefine common marketplace definitions
- Can introduce new categories of solutions

> **Sample Generic Solution**
> *The Solution: Supply Consolidation and Automation*
> Supply consolidation and automation can overcome the challenges of handling supplies, resulting in a highly efficient supply chain that returns greater profits to the hospital operating room. *Supply consolidation* is the grouping of many single items into larger packages or kits for better supply chain efficiency. For example, when supplies for a particular type of procedure are grouped into a kit, a single package can be easily ordered, billed, stored and repurchased. *Supply automation* is the use of technology to streamline inventory, consumption, charging and ordering procedures. For example, secure cabinetry, bar code technology and radio-frequency devices enable the tracking of items throughout the supply chain, helping management identify the status of supplies and inventory.

The Components of Generic Solutions

The generic solution discussion usually follows the problem development or historical overview portions of your white paper.

Not every white paper is an ideal candidate for a generic solution discussion. Technical papers would usually bypass this generic discussion.

To begin with, generic solution discussions will NEVER mention a company name or a product name. They should also avoid using company-branding elements, such as slogans or trademarked phrases. Rather, generic solutions define a category or "bucket," in which a solution lives. The description should be easy to understand and product-agnostic.

Some companies have zero competition and thus have never considered defining an industry category for their solution. Other businesses have developed products that redefine an existing category. Regardless of where your solution fits into the world of possible options, it CAN be described generically.

Begin by brainstorming what you might want to name your generic solution. For example, consider a product that is essentially a mobile phone at its core, but adds the ability to receive television broadcasts. From a marketing perspective, it might be wise to define a new category called TV phones, mobile entertainment devices or personal media assistants. Even if you are the second, third or sixtieth company bringing a similar product to market, you can redefine the marketplace by focusing in on your solution in a generic way that differentiates it from other categorical descriptions.

A real-world example is electronic paper. Briefly, e-paper is a new display technology that simply produces black and white output. Some smart folks decided to call it e-paper because it is very thin and does not require a constant stream of power to display information. Even though the technology was first developed in the 1970s, it was not until Sony introduced an e-paper reader in 2006 that the "category" has been defined as "new."

In highly competitive markets, it might make sense to slightly extend an existing, well-known category. For example, if some small competitor to Microsoft takes the word processor to a whole new level, they might define it as second-generation word processing, a next-generation word processor or some other slight alteration from the accepted phrase.

When you create your generic solution, consider the following:

Define the category: When defining a category, simply explain what the product is and what it does rather than focusing exclusively on its benefits (we will do that later). For example, a TV phone could simply be a mobile device that combines television and wireless phone services. Be sure to speak in terms that relate to your ideal reader. If you are targeting cellular engineers, you might want a more detailed description than if you are targeting a retail purchasing agents.

Add nuance: When you define the solution, be sure to differentiate it from alternatives. Back to the TV phone, you could explain that it contains a built-in receiver to enable the reception of all local television shows, just like a regular TV. This might help clarify how it differs from the phones that offer video download services.

Explain what it is: You know your solution so well that you might be tempted to overlook a very simple description of what it actually is. With the TV phone, is it a mobile hardware device, an add-on to existing mobile phones or something displayed on your television? Take nothing for granted. If you sell a software solution, is it a plug-in to a platform, a web-based application or a client-side application? Be specific when explaining the solution, but be careful not to slide into details about the actual product you are selling.

Defining a New Category

You can always define a category that does not exist in your marketplace. This is a tricky process. For example, if your industry understands and accepts a specific term or phrase, you might not want to swim upstream with something new.

Alternatively, if your product is first to market, you have the opportunity to speak of the category as if it previously existed. This is valuable because you can set the standard terms in your market and because it helps remove the perception of "new and untested." Furthermore, you have the opportunity to define the key characteristics of your new category.

When developing a new category, try not to be too narrow or too broad in your description. Keep your target readers in mind. Be sure that the words you pick to define the category have staying power. Certain words rise like a tidal wave into popular phraseology and then disappear as if they never existed.

BENEFITS

Benefits address the "so what," "who cares," and "what's in it for me" nature of every person. Benefits are persuasive rather than descriptive and must be relevant to your readers. Because most white papers try to persuade, it is wise to discuss benefits in a solution-agnostic manner. When you focus on the benefits of the generic solution rather than your specific product, you remove the perception of overt selling.

If you adopt a problem-solution approach to your white paper, the benefits should be directly related to the problems you put forth. All white papers can and should address benefits. Even a highly technical white paper should be sure to include a discussion of the benefits of a process or technology.

Why Benefits Matter

Benefits turn people on, waking them from their slumber. They address needs in a direct manner. If your back hurts from typing all day long at your keyboard and you see something that says, "Eliminates writers' back pain," that will most certainly grab your attention. I am easily distracted when I write. If there were a little pill that, "Purges all distractions for up to 3 hours," you can bet I would be first in line to purchase it.

We live in a benefits-driven society. Everyone wants to know "why" but is often afraid to ask. Benefits are direct and bring home the advantage of a product, service or process. Here are some advantages of clearly stated benefits:

- Persuades your reader
- Demonstrates you have considered your reader's needs
- Provides tangible reasons to work with you and your company
- Explains why your solution matters
- Arms readers with information to help them persuade others

Features versus Benefits

Benefits differ from features in a few significant ways. The feature is a description of a tangible attribute of a product or service. For example, a GPS locator might be a feature of a mobile phone. The feature by itself is not very attractive or compelling without a benefit.

A benefit is an advantage of a feature, product or service. For example, the benefit of GPS might be the ability to add mapping programs to a phone or being quickly located in the case of an emergency. The benefit addresses a need and the feature describes how the need is delivered.

Discussing benefits is an acquired skill, much as the enjoyment of beer is an acquired taste. Often the words *features* and *benefits* are used hand-and-hand, as if they are one and the same. In reality, benefits must come before features—a counterintuitive position for many people. Once someone has been persuaded they "need" what you have to offer, a natural next step is to want to know the product's features. Sell first and worry about features and functions later. For companies selling technical products, this is difficult to swallow because so many technology companies have relied on feature-based selling.

Let's further distinguish between a feature and a benefit. If your paper is about LED-based nightlights, you might be inclined to discuss their tiny form factor, bulb-free design and unique brightness. To translate those very same features into benefits, simply ask yourself, "Why do these features matter to my reader?" Rethought, you might state that LED nightlights are safe to place anywhere, never need replacement bulbs and emit significantly more light than traditional nightlights. You will notice that these benefits are notably more compelling than their associated features.

The following list outlines a few features and their feasible benefits. It should be noted that a single feature could have many different benefits.

Feature	Benefit
Multi-sourced data analysis	Validate credit card information with greater accuracy
Push-to-talk mobile communications	Simplify the coordination of a mobile workforce
Geographical ad targeting	Assure online advertisements are displayed only to prospects who live in specific regions
E-mail automation	Speed response time to frequently asked questions
Concrete siding	Permanently eliminate the need to paint the exterior of your home
Video on-demand	Enable consumers to watch what they want, when they want

You will notice that the benefits samples above were written so they could stand on their own, without any mention of the specific feature. For more detail on translating features into benefits, see Chapter 9. With strong benefits, a white paper could simply mention the benefits and NEVER need to mention features. If the benefit resonates with the reader's needs and addresses the problems you outlined earlier in your white paper, it will help drive the reader toward the goal.

The Components of a Benefits Section

At its core, discussing benefits is basic salesmanship.
As in selling, it is critical to write to the right reader. If
your ideal reader is the marketing director and you begin
discussing benefits that only an engineer would appre-
ciate, you have lost your way. It is wise to go back to your
initial needs assessment and reexamine the goals and
ideal reader when writing this section of your white paper
(see Chapter 2).

When coming up with a list of benefits, start by examining the problems you have identified in your outline
(see Chapter 3). Each problem might be overcome by your
solution in multiple ways, forming an initial list of benefits.

After you have come up with benefits that address
every key problem, you should also consider related
benefits that might not have an associated problem. For
example, if a key challenge was the poor viewing angle of
existing laptop screens and your solution's key benefit
is doubling the acceptable viewing angle, you might also
mention that the solution reduces eyestrain.

The formulation of a benefits statement is rather
simple. Lead with an action verb, such as:

- Improves
- Enhances
- Extends
- Assures
- Validates
- Delivers
- Maximizes
- Enables
- Reduces
- Frees
- Simplifies
- Provides
- Blocks

Follow the verb with some descriptive text that directly addresses a problem. Among the possible classifications of benefits, there are three primary categories: business, technical and process benefits.

Business benefits: These benefits discuss how the solution helps improve things from a business perspective. For example, if the topic was instant messaging, the benefit might be, "Enables employees to instantly communicate across the country at a very low cost."

Technical benefits: Benefits that are more technical address some of the detailed advantages of a solution. Again using instant messaging, an example might include, "Supports all major computer operating systems."

Process benefits: A process benefit examines how a solution improves existing processes. With the instant messaging example, a process benefit might include, "Automatically and effortlessly stores all customer communications for federal regulatory compliance."

The benefits section of your white paper can be simply formatted. Often, a short opening statement might introduce the benefits section. A bulleted list of benefits could be the remainder of this section.

You can add more meat to your benefits by discussing the implications of each benefit to your readers. To come up with an implication to a benefit, simply ask yourself, "Why does that matter to my ideal reader?" For example, the instant messaging benefit, "Supports all major computer operating systems," could be expanded to include, "ensuring all users are able to participate in instant messaging" or "enabling older or outdated systems to benefit from instant messaging."

THE "WHAT TO LOOK FOR" LIST

We live in a "do it yourself" society. When it's time to try something new and outside your area of expertise, you most likely seek advice. Similarly, people read white papers to learn before they leap. Why not use your white paper to provide valuable advice to seekers?

Establishing a "key considerations" or "what to look for when seeking a solution" list is a very valuable service to your readers. In reality, this section is the most powerful and persuasive element of the entire white paper because you have the opportunity to set the bar against which your competition will be judged. This list is especially critical for white papers that are business benefits focused.

Why "What to Look for" Lists?

The unique advantage of providing advice lies in the way it is delivered. Often, readers have a limited under-standing when discerning good from poor, especially if your solution is new to them. By providing a list of key considerations, you are essentially telling readers how to shop for YOUR solution, without ever mentioning your product. The list should be written in such a way that it leads readers down a path, at the end of which only your solution stands.

Objective lists of key considerations offer the following advantages:

- Provides a valuable buyer's guide to readers
- Eliminates the competition
- Introduces your specific advantages without directly calling them out
- Translates certain features into "must-haves"
- Allows you to position the "type of company" a prospect should be searching for
- Demonstrates your expertise

Sample "What to Look for"
What to Look for in a White Paper Writer
Finding the right person to write a white paper is NOT a simple task. Here are a few things to look for:

- **Writing skills:** Is this person generally good at writing? Has he or she done a significant amount of it? Will he or she be open to suggestions and changes?
- **Interviewing skills:** Can the writer efficiently extract the key nuggets of information from content experts—information necessary to write an effective paper? A good white paper writer is similar to a journalist, asking the important questions that reveal the key points of a paper.
- **Experience with white papers:** Now that you have found a writer, can he or she do white papers? It takes a specialized breed to truly understand the idiosyncrasies that make a white paper great. Be sure to ask for white paper samples.
- **Technical competency:** Can the writer bridge the gap between what engineers are saying and the language spoken by the reader? This requires a general technical competency and a good understanding of the target audience.
- **Organized and motivated:** Pigeonholing thoughts into clearly organized categories is essential for a white paper writer. Good organization should be driven by a motivation to do the work and see it through to completion.

The Components of a "What to Look for" List

This portion of your white paper must be carefully crafted and placed. To maximize its persuasive power, it should be located somewhere before the specific introduction of your solution. Why? Because after you have revealed the details of your solution, readers will see such a list with a different set of lenses and might even ignore it.

The list must be fully objective and should not include specific references to names or features that are associated with your company or product. For example, if you are IBM, avoid saying "Work with IBM" or some other known brand that is associated only with IBM. Rather, you could say, "Work with an established leader..." and describe why that is so important.

Remember your ideal reader when writing this portion of your white paper. Tailor the list to that specific person. This is your chance to persuade, so stay focused on your goal of getting through to that ideal reader.

Do not try to make the list all-encompassing. Rather, come up with key considerations that differentiate you from your competition and focus in on those particulars. A good rule of thumb is to limit the list to no more than 10 items.

When formulating your list, it is always helpful to team up with someone who sells the product or service for a living. This person can help establish some compelling "what to look for" items for your list.

There are two primary categories that should be considered for any "what to look for" list:

Product features: If your solution has a few unique product advantages over the competition, it is very wise to call out those features as key considerations. For example, if your company produced a commercial paint applicator that reduces paint overspray, you might say, "Look for a paint applicator that transfers at least 90 percent of paint to targeted surfaces." You could go on to explain that this capability reduces the need for multiple coats of paint and speeds the entire process.

Type of company: It is wise to talk about the type of company your reader should be seeking. If you are a large business, you could focus on terms like, "Seek an experienced vendor who can support your needs as they change." If you are a startup business, you might say,

"Look for a company that leverages the latest technology and is agile enough to meet your custom requirements." Other standard corporate considerations might include what type of service offerings to look for, asking about established clientele and working with a company that has been operating in the marketplace for a number of years.

USING EXAMPLES

Whether hypothetical or actual, providing examples can be a compelling addition to your white paper. You will notice that this book is littered with many examples.

Examples apply what has previously been discussed in your white paper to probable scenarios. They describe processes with words and are often enhanced with illustrations. Examples can also provide readers a demonstration of how your solution might work. A word of caution: Comprehensive examples can also provide more detail than is necessary for your white paper and may turn off your readers. Tread lightly.

Examples are often applied after the benefits section of white papers and in the context of a generic description of your solution. If the solution is rather complex and confusing, it might be wise to provide multiple examples and introduce them as early as possible. Examples can also be used after you have described your specific solution. In these cases, your example can address real clients or real scenarios that you want associated with your brand.

Why Examples Matter

Especially powerful for technical papers, examples demonstrate a process in an easy-to-understand manner. Examples also help build affinity with your readers. If your audience relates to your examples, you have strengthened your case.

Examples provide the following unique advantages:

- Illustrate a process and how it works
- Create usage scenarios that can be tailored for different audiences
- Draw pictures with words
- Clarify your offering
- Build reader affinity

Multimedia Message Example
Multimedia messaging is expected to be a popular mobile application. With a multimodal-enabled mobile device, users will be able to combine verbal commands and onscreen visuals to send and receive multimedia messages. For example, a user will be able to ask her phone to display new mail by simply saying, "Open mail." The user can specify a message to open by saying something such as, "Open Judy's mail." If a multimedia message has a picture attached, the user can simply say, "View picture." The entire process is performed hands-free, combining voice recognition, onscreen graphics and text displays.

The Components of an Example

You might be inclined to simply drop in some preexisting case studies and customer quotes in this portion of your white paper. Avoid the temptation. Actual case studies and quotes from customers are overt marketing materials. When you add them to your white paper, you remind readers you are trying to sell something, essentially shifting them from education and soft-sell into a gear that might encourage them to abandon the rest of your white paper.

Rather, consider using case studies as a basis for an example. Instead of describing how Dell benefited from your solution, discuss how a leading computer manufacturer was able to accomplish some key objectives. Alternatively, describe how computer manufacturers in general might use your solution. This avoids the need to gain client approval for mentioning their specific company in your white paper (a slow process) and focuses more on the example and less on the client. Near the end of the white paper, consider offering readers case studies to motivate them to contact the company for more information.

It should be stated that examples do not need to live in a distinct place in your white paper. Rather, they can be scattered throughout the document and integrated into existing sections, adding strength wherever they are needed.

When you provide examples, adding illustrations and screen shots are very helpful, especially for technical processes. Often, a visual representation of a process is much easier to follow than many paragraphs of text. You should make sure to avoid extraneous information that is outside your topic area or lacks context. Many technical diagrams include more details than are needed to convey their point. Try to keep it simple.

THE SPECIFIC SOLUTION

Now we have come to the place where you CAN talk about your solution—finally! When you get to the specific solution discussion, you are removing your veil and disclosing the salesperson behind the curtain. This is where you DO talk about your product and your company.

Discussing the specific solution signifies that the end of the paper is near. By this point, you have extensively educated, directed and persuaded your reader. You have introduced the problems, talked about key market drivers, generically defined the solution, discussed its benefits and provided "what to look for" guidance. If you have done things right, your ideal reader will be well persuaded and interested in finding out about your specific offering.

Why Specific Solutions Matter

It's almost a no-brainer that a discussion about your actual product, service or idea should be mentioned in the white paper. Most white papers ONLY focus on the specific solution and skip everything else discussed in this book. Including a section about your solution should be the simplest part of the white paper and should resonate with most writers.

However, some extremists believe that a white paper must purely educate and never sell. Such logic is questionable. The effort, energy and persuasive power of white papers should be channeled to your advantage. By fully avoiding the mention of your company or solution, all you do is provide general goodwill to your readers, but leave them questioning where to go to acquire such a product or implement such a concept.

Introducing the specifics about your solution provides a number of advantages, including:

- Ties a tangible product or service to your reader's problems
- Helps drive the branding of your company and your specific offering
- Starts the sales process
- Wraps ups the document

Sample Specific Solution
Reasons to Partner With Stelzner Consulting for Your White Paper Needs
This paper merely touches the surface of the art of white paper writing. If you need help completing your white paper, need one updated or want someone to produce multiple papers with a common flavor, consider Stelzner Consulting. We bring the following advantages to your project:

Extensive writing experience: Stelzner Consulting has mastered the art of white paper writing as evidenced by our extensive online portfolio and highly successful educational articles. We have written for *Fortune 500* companies and many emerging organizations.

Proven process: Each white paper project includes a comprehensive needs assessment, custom outline development, extensive interviews, a detailed review of your solution, research on your competitors and your industry, skillful writing, support illustrations, layout development, editorial review and revisions.

Rave reviews: Many of our clients engage us for follow-on writing projects, a sign of our quality.

We do the hard work: We ask the right questions, drive the entire process and lead you down the path to success.

Extensively published: Our papers have received international acclaim. Leading universities use them as required reading.

Direct access to high-level writers: Only senior-level writers with at least 10 years experience will be working on your white paper.

(continued)

Broad technology experience: Stelzner Consulting
has written on topics ranging from artificial intelligence to e-mail spam. Market expertise includes
software, networking, storage, security, hardware,
medical, wireless and the Internet.

Comprehensive needs assessment: By asking the
right questions up front, we assure your paper is
focused on the appropriate audience and your objectives are achieved.

Editorial review: Every paper is reviewed by
an independent editor before you see the first
draft. This important quality control is a Stelzner
Consulting distinction.

The Components of a Specific Solution Discussion

Remember the purpose of your white paper. If your paper
is a business-benefits piece, its goal is to take the soft-
sell approach. Thus, the specific solution should simply
tease the reader with enough information so he or she
will want to contact the company and enter the sales
cycle. However, with technical white papers, it is very
appropriate to go into details about the solution.

When you introduce your solution, be explicit about
what it is. A successful formula includes linking the solution to the previous sections of the paper, introducing the
company and identifying the solution's unique advantages.

Connect the solution to previous sections: Start by
explaining that your solution meets all of the requirements outlined in the prior sections of the white paper
(especially if you have a "What to Look for" section).
Explain in detail your product's relationship to the

general category you defined (see "The Generic Solution" section earlier in this chapter). Consider the following fictitious example, "An advanced TV phone, the TakeTV device unifies mobile phone and television services into a single handheld unit, enabling users to receive both phone calls and local TV reception."

Introduce the company: If you previously wrote about key considerations when selecting a company, be sure to address some of those issues here. For example, if you mentioned, "Seek a business with at least a decade of experience," you might say something like this: "Established in the mid-1990s, the TakeTV product is designed and developed by On-The-Go Mobile Communications, Inc., a recognized leader in converging mobile and entertainment communications."

Mention some advantages: Discuss some of the unique advantages and features your solution brings to ideal readers. An advantage is a statement that differentiates your solution from the competition. A feature can qualify as an advantage. Earlier in the white paper, you should have mentioned the generic benefits of your product. Try not to repeat those benefits here. Rather, expand on them in more depth or include added benefits and features that the reader might find valuable. For example, "TakeTV not only clearly receives local TV signals, it also enables users to pause and rewind broadcast video, ensuring they never miss an important moment."

As a rule of thumb, try not to write more than a few pages about your specific solution. If your white paper is 6 to 12 pages in length, allocate only a page or two to the specific product and company. You most likely could dedicate the entire paper to a specific discussion of your product or solution. However, if you did that, you would essentially be creating a large product brochure and not a persuasive white paper. The only exception would be if you were describing a rather complex technical concept.

In the case of a business-benefits or thought leadership piece, the bulk of the white paper should set the need and describe the solution generically.

CONCLUDE WITH A CALL TO ACTION

The very last words of your white paper should guide a reader to take a well-thought-out and intentional action. Providing a clear next step will help the reader enter into your sales cycle, provide him or her more information or accomplish just about any other task you wish. However, avoiding a clear, actionable next step will result in the filing of your white paper, perhaps in the dreaded circular file!

Why a Call to Action Matters

Providing an actionable step that guides readers when they reach the end of your white paper helps keep the prospect engaged with your solution. In the marketing world, this is referred to as a *call to action*. A call to action directs a user to act in some way.

The call to action takes its roots in the traditional world of advertising. Open a magazine or simply look in your e-mail inbox and you will find a cornucopia of examples. Some might include:

- Visit your local dealer to test drive a car
- Visit our luxury vacation property and receive a one-night complementary stay
- Visit our website for more information
- Call now to receive a free life insurance quote

> **Sample Call to Action: VistaPrint**
> *Our Offer to You: FREE 250 Business Cards!*
> Over 5 million small businesses and consumers have already chosen VistaPrint for everything from business cards and brochures to postcards and letterhead. To help you kick off your marketing efforts, VistaPrint would like to ship you **250 full-color business cards FREE with no further obligation** (all you pay is shipping and handling). You can design and place your order in as few as five minutes!
>
> Visit www.vistaprint.com/smallbusiness today to choose your professionally printed cards from 42 full-color designs and start down the VistaPrint road to business success.[6]
>
> ---
> [6] VistaPrint. (2005). Marketing your business on a shoestring budget: A practical guide to success. See http://www.vistaprintsmallbusiness.com.

The above VistaPrint call to action was part of a comprehensive white paper campaign. In only 60 days, VistaPrint had 5,000 people register for its white paper, and more than 10 percent converted into a sale.[7] This compelling call to action played a big role in converting readers into buyers. A free offer was provided to entice readers to view free and for-purchase VistaPrint products.

The Components of a Call to Action

The very last words in your white paper should encourage every reader to act. The call must be clear, provide an advantage for acting and explicitly state how the reader

---

[7] Hartsock, N. (December 2005). *WhitePaperSource*. Major online print company uses educational white paper to drive permission-based marketing, http://www.whitepapersource.com/marketing/casestudy-vistaprint.html.

should take the next step. The possible actions are many, including:

- Purchasing a product
- Registering for a newsletter
- Scheduling an appointment
- Visiting a website
- Calling a sales representative
- Offering access to special content
- Providing a coupon or discount

According Michelle Keegan, an e-mail-marketing expert, a good call to action must be visible, clear, compelling, urgent and direct.[8] Let's explore each of these attributes:

Visible: You can make the call to action stand out by simply enclosing it in a colored box to draw attention to it. In addition, you can boldface certain keywords to bring emphasis.

Clear: Keegan explains the action step must be easy to read and contain just a few sentences. Be clear about what you are providing. Rather than simply saying, "Visit our website for details," try "Visit www.YourName.com/ offer/ for access to special reports and comprehensive case studies."

Compelling: Provide something of value that will encourage your reader to want to take another step closer to your company. Be sure to include action-oriented language, such as "visit today," "act now," or "gain instant access."

Urgent: If your white paper is designed to generate leads, you want those leads flowing in quickly. You can create a sense of urgency by offering a limited-time offer or a special to readers who respond within a few days of receiving the white paper.

---

[8] Keegan, M. (May 2, 2003). Get more clicks with a good call-to-action, http://www.constantcontact.com/e-mail-marketing-resources/hints-tips/volume6-issue6.jsp.

Direct: Point your readers to the exact place you want them to go. You can set up a special tracking URL on your website to gauge the success of your call to action. Consider building a custom webpage for the white paper call to action and track its hits and sales conversions. If you are distributing the white paper electronically as a PDF file, hyperlink the web address in your PDF file to make it easy for folks to get to the offer.

ABOUT SUMMARIES

Most white papers do not have a summary or conclusion. Generally, magazine articles do not include a summary. Neither do brochures. You might find a summary or closing thoughts in some non-fiction books. However, white papers do not typically include a traditional summary or conclusion that rehashes what the reader just learned. Because the average white paper is fewer than 12 pages in length and combines the attributes of an article and a brochure, it makes sense to end with a call to action for the reader, rather than a summary.

However, if you are determined to include a summary, briefly restate your solution and be sure you address how it overcomes the key challenges faced by the reader (as set forth in your outline). Try to keep the summary to a few paragraphs and avoid the terms "summary" or "conclusion." Rather, try these headers: "Closing Thoughts" or "The Last Word," which are less formal and are more likely to be examined by your reader.

This chapter provided a deep dive into the many core components of a white paper. The following chapter will provide helpful information for the writer seeking general writing guidance, such as how to translate features into benefits and writing when you are not the content expert.

✻ Chapter 9 ✻

Writing Tips and Strategies

"When you write, try to leave out all the parts readers skip."

—Elmore Leonard

In this chapter, you will find a mix of valuable tips and strategies that will help you strengthen your writing. If you are an engineer, a freelancer, a marketing professional, a project manager, a student or are new to business-to-business writing, this chapter is for you. If you are a seasoned writer, you might simply want to skim the following pages for some new ideas.

This chapter covers tips on converting features into benefits, writing when you are not the expert, the creative use of quotations, common writing traps, how to overcome writer's block and the value of hiring an editor.

TRANSLATING FEATURES INTO BENEFITS

Writing to persuade is a craft that differs from writing to inform. Many journalists and technical writers are proficient writers and excel at telling stories and informing their readers. However, there is a distinction between an informative piece and a persuasive one. Most white papers are clearly persuasive documents first and informative pieces second. A key component of any persuasive document is a discussion of benefits. The benefits address the "why" value proposition. For an in-depth examination of benefits, be sure to look at the "Benefits" section of Chapter 8.

I came from the world of technical product marketing. At first, my job was to convey features and functions. That task was not very difficult. However, when management began asking me to think about benefits, I really struggled at first. I lacked any clear guidance and had some significant misses in the early years.

I learned that the key to distinguishing between a feature and a benefit is to ask, "Does this statement have an explicitly stated value to my ideal reader?" The value must be clearly called out in words AND it must be accurate, important and relevant to your readers. An integrated spell-checker in a word processor is clearly not a benefit because there is no explicitly stated value. However, the added assurance that a project will not have spelling errors is a benefit.

Converting a feature into a benefit starts by asking questions. Let's work through a hypothetical example. A large company that makes printers and scanners is adding a new feature that scans transparent media, such as slides and film. Is slide scanning a feature or a benefit? It depends how you say it. By itself, a slide scanner is a feature. However, by adding a few words, it starts to take the form of a benefit. For example, "Able to instantly scan slides" is a benefit, albeit a weak one. If you want to develop the benefit further, ask the following questions:

- Who is using the feature?
- Why would someone need that feature?
- What problem is the feature solving?
- What are people saying about the feature and why do they like it?
- What is the implication of that feature?
- Why does the feature matter to our readers?

Let's say you learn that the ideal readers are small-business photographers who are converting film negatives from analog to digital. One problem might be the current lack of a quick and easy way to perform conversions without sending negatives to a photo-processing lab. Thus, a benefit of the slide scanner might be, "Dramatically speeds the conversion of film to a digital file," or "Eliminates costly third-party scanning requirements."

Notice that the mention of slide scanning has been done away with in the benefits sentence. Why? It is not the slide scanner that is valuable, it is what the slide scanner can do or how it can improve someone's work that is a truly powerful benefit.

WRITING WHEN YOU ARE *NOT* THE EXPERT

How can you write about something when you have little or no topical expertise? The good news is a good writer can write about anything and an expert is typically not the best person to be writing a white paper.

The art of writing is actually translation. If you can take a challenging topic and distill it into palatable words that your reader can understand, you are well on your way. I have written about some of the most challenging topics, ranging from artificial intelligence to surgical equipment sanitation. If I can do this, so can you. With the exception of legal and ultra-scientific topics, there's no reason why a capable writer could not write a white paper on nearly any topic.

The challenge is being perceived as an expert by your ideal reader. How can you write so a niche reader—say, CEO of a manufacturer or a director of marketing at a major retailer—thinks you know your stuff; even if you have zero experience in manufacturing or marketing?

The answer lies in your ability to ask questions and perform research. If you have access to experts and are meticulous about your project, you will most certainly be closer to the goal.

The first key is to clearly identify your ideal reader, down to an actual job title and type of business (see Chapter 2 for a detailed discussion of the needs assessment). If you do your job right, you will end up with something very specific, such as an IT manager working for a small business in the financial services industry that is relying on Microsoft SharePoint Portal Server. Once you know who to write to, you are heading down the right path.

The next step is to have direct access to content specialists. These experts tend to wear different hats depending on the size of your business or client. For example, the content expert might be a product manager, a sales director, an engineer, an executive or an outside analyst. Once you have clearly defined a key expert or two, use those experts as your sounding board throughout the entire process.

Be sure to ask your expert for recommended reading to ramp up your knowledge on the topic. This may include existing white papers or articles from a few trade publication websites. Ask about key descriptive words or catch-phrases that are used in the industry by your ideal reader.

For example, if you are writing about liposuction, ask whether the titles *plastic surgeon, cosmetic surgeon* or simply *doctor* are preferred most by readers. The key here is to use terms in a way that would be appropriate if you were actually the expert writing to your peers.

As you go through the process of establishing your outline, be sure to have it approved and sanitized by your content expert. Walk through that outline verbally with the expert and ask him or her, "Will this resonate with our target readers?" Experts are often busy and like to process things over e-mail. It is important to get one-on-one time with these folks and ask them to carefully consider if your points are relevant.

As you begin your interviewing process, it is wise to talk to actual customers who are the ideal readers. If you arrange time with them on the phone, you should explain that you are not an expert on the topic and want to ask them some questions related to their expertise. Most times, if you can gain access to customers, they will be thrilled to talk to you. You can use their comments to add strength to your document. Also, consider asking them to review your draft.

When you perform your research, be sure to read many articles and papers that were written to the same target reader. This will help you understand the common language used when writing to this type of person. You also might want to look at a competitor's solution for valuable context.

The review cycle will be critical. Make sure all of your experts spend quality time examining your paper for relevancy to the target reader. Do not be disappointed when they suggest changes. By following these simple steps, your paper will appear as if it was written by a topical expert.

USING QUOTES TO STRENGTHEN YOUR PAPER

Using third-party quotes and citations is a very powerful and compelling way to add validity and strength to your white paper.

Information that is from a published source, such as a trade magazine, analyst report or journal should be closely examined. After you have performed all of your research and read everything, you should end up with many highlighted pages of notes. When you find a good quote, consider using it in your white paper and citing the source.

Quotes can be used in a variety of creative ways. For example, imagine you are writing about identity theft. Let's examine the following quote from an old Gartner Group press release:

> "More than half of all identity theft—where the method of theft is documented—is committed by

criminals that have established relationships with their victims, such as family members, roommates, neighbors, or co-workers," said Avivah Litan, vice president and research director for Gartner, citing numbers published by the Federal Trade Commission.[1]

There are many ways to use this excellent quote, as follows:

Complete citation: You could simply quote Litan, stating precisely what was said and adding value to your paper by citing a recognized analyst.

Partial Citation: Consider simplifying the citation by stating that Litan says, "More than half of all identity theft—where the method of theft is documented—is committed by criminals that have established relationships with their victims." Not mentioning the part about family members and roommates might strengthen your point if you are focusing on workplace identity theft.

Paraphrase: You could say: Most identity-theft crimes initiate among friends and acquaintances, states Gartner analyst Avivah Litan. Alternatively, you could say: The Federal Trade Commission found that people we already know, such as neighbors and co-workers, commit the majority of identity-theft crimes.

By simply taking the parts that will further your cause and leaving the rest behind, you can significantly strengthen your paper. The trick is locating the golden nuggets among the pages of your research and keeping your citations accurate to the intention of the original author.

WRITING TRAPS: WHAT TO AVOID

Below are some of the more common mistakes that should be avoided when writing white papers:

---

[1] See http://www.gartner.com/5_about/press_releases/pr21july2003a.jsp.

Early self-promotion: Avoid addressing your solution in a specific manner early in your white paper. This means keep the specific solution out of the first few paragraphs and even the first few pages. When you explain your specific product or service right away, you send the message that the white paper is a sales document and discourage the reader from going further with your piece. Rather, start with a problem discussion and only hint generically at the solution.

Irrelevant content: Including extraneous information just because it is interesting or sounds good is akin to a taxicab driver stopping to talk to a friend while you are in the car. Your readers' time is very valuable and they are not obligated to read your white paper. Compel them to read your document by keeping EVERYTHING you write highly relevant to their needs, interests and challenges.

Long prose: Short is good. Long sentences are very hard to track because they require the reader stay engaged for a very long time, ultimately boring the reader to death and increasing the likelihood he or she will abandon the document, fall asleep or otherwise find your paper boring, a situation you surely want to avoid. Did you notice that the second sentence dragged you along?

Long blocks of text: As a general rule, try to avoid writing more than three or four paragraphs before you introduce some writing gimmick that makes it easy for the reader to jump along through your white paper. For example, a subhead, photo, illustration, bulleted list, table or chart will help the reader stay connected to your document. No-one likes seeing pages of endless paragraphs.

Lack of flow: Your white paper should be like one of those lazy rivers at a water park, effortlessly flowing readers along. Be sure to use transitions between major sections. Stay topically relevant. For example, if you have a section on history, do not use that section to discuss the benefits of your solution.

Humor: Long jokes and wit should be avoided in the white paper, especially in the beginning. White papers are respected and serious documents that are used to make important decisions.

OVERCOMING WRITER'S BLOCK

I have a confession. I regularly suffer from serious writer's block. This is something that frankly never fully disappears, even with extensive writing experience. I know many people are blessed and never seem to have a problem getting their ideas down in writing. Because I have struggled with writer's block for some time, I am well-qualified to provide some tips to help you manage your writer's block.

You know you have writer's block if you would rather do almost anything else but write. Do you sit down at the keyboard, ready to start, and this little voice in your head whispers, "Maybe you should check your e-mail," "Don't forget to call your friend back," or beckons you to some other more desirable task?

Writer's block tends to be brought on by a few key issues. First, there seems to be no sense of urgency for a project. Second, you are allowing other things to dictate your daily schedule and priorities, such as your incoming e-mail. Third, you have too much on your mind and are not sure how to clear it. Fourth, you lack the self-confidence to believe you can actually write something acceptable—even if you are regularly praised for your writing. Fifth, you are a perfectionist and because nothing is ever done right, you never get around to writing. The list goes on and on, but you get the point.

Be sure to examine "Preparation for Writing" in Chapter 6 for tips and ideas on how to get ready to write. Here are some ideas to help you overcome your writer's block:

Identify your productivity zones. There are certain times of the day where you are much more productive than others. Figure out when they are and be sure to write during those time slots. This tip alone will dramatically enhance your ability to document your words.

Get up one hour earlier: When you need to write a white paper, try setting your alarm for one hour earlier than normal. Dedicate your newfound time exclusively to writing your white paper. You will be surprised how well your body adapts to one less hour of sleep. This tip was key to helping me produce this book.

Turn off the world: Shut off all external distractions. This means kill your e-mail, your instant messaging application, your cell phone, your desk phone or anything else that could distract you. Shut your door and ask not to be disturbed. Try some classical music to drown out any sounds.

Quickly document your thoughts: Don't worry about how it sounds; just get your words down. Start writing and get those fingers moving. Come back later, refine your writing and make it sound better.

Change your setting: Try going for a walk. Take a pen and paper with you. See if your mind is cleared or if new ideas come to you that encourage you to write.

Accomplish smaller tasks regularly: Try working on smaller portions of the white paper each day. For example, make a goal of completing one page each day. When the task is manageable and achievable, you will find your way to the end quickly.

Reward yourself when you write: Set some milestones and reward yourself with a nice lunch, a trip to Starbucks or some other indulgence AFTER you have accomplished a major goal in your white paper.

Do a little research: As you begin surfing the web and finding valuable bits of information to enhance your white paper, you might be encouraged to begin writing.

USING AN EDITOR

Hiring a professional editor can move your white paper from great to excellent. Even if you are a well-refined writer, you will miss glaring mistakes in your writing.

The best way to see if you could benefit from an editor is to let your work rest for a day or two and reexamine it. As you read it, do you see problems you never seemed to have noticed before? The fact is that many writers are constantly cranking out work and often lack the critical and objective eye that an editor brings to a project.

Having an editor is a small expense that will ensure your work is refined and free from errors that could tarnish your credibility or the image of your company. Writers often become so familiar and enamored with their own work that they never notice their own mistakes. An insignificant error could damage a writer's credibility or make him or her appear sloppy.

If you are a freelance writer, an investment in an editor is a wise move. It will help ensure nothing goes to the client with serious problems and will increase your perceived value by stating you have an added quality assurance layer in place.

Editors provide a variety of services ranging from simple grammar-checking and sentence structure to fact-checking. A very skilled editor will be able to suggest better ways to write a sentence, identify improper word use, suggest ways to restructure certain sections, and the list goes on. A good editor will find content-specific errors that Microsoft Word could never identify.

An editor can improve the strength of your white paper in the following ways:

- Making sure your verbs are compelling
- Cutting unnecessary words
- Checking grammar, spelling and punctuation
- Assuring your style is consistent
- Verifying the spelling of business names and terms
- Identifying unclear or confusing statements
- Pointing out formatting inconsistencies
- Testing web addresses
- Locating the inconsistent use of proper names

Here are a few tips to qualifying an editor. First, examine the person's education and work experience. While it is true that many people claim to be editors, few truly specialize in it as their trade. Ask for some samples of cdited projects and for references on those very same projects. When speaking to references, ask how quickly the editor completed the project and how the overall experience has been.

If you write a lot and need a regular editor, Lisa Hernandez of Editorial and Production Services (see Appendix III for editors) recommends a test project. Take an existing document and insert some basic errors, such as misspellings, repeated words, incorrect punctuation, subject/verb disagreements, spelling a person's name two different ways and inserting a broken web link. Track what you have changed and see what the editor catches. A good editor will catch everything.

Be sure to have your editor track his or her changes in Microsoft Word. When you receive the edited document, you do not need to accept every suggestion. However, you will notice, that a good editor ALWAYS finds something that could be improved with your white paper.

This chapter provided some valuable tips and strategies to improve your white paper writing. The presentation of your words on paper is also important. The following chapter will discuss the formatting of your white paper.

❋ Chapter 10 ❋

Formatting the White Paper

"It's all right to have butterflies in your stomach. Just get them to fly in formation."

—Dr. Rob Gilbert

The visual appearance of a white paper is just as important as the actual words you write. To pull readers into a white paper, it should be visually appealing.

If you look at enough white papers, you will begin to see they share common formatting. Usually, white papers use generous white space—the area around the text—and include light graphical treatments.

White papers should avoid the overuse of graphical elements. If they approach the higher-end look and feel of a brochure, white papers will lose their perception as educational pieces and instead be viewed as marketing or sales documents by your readers. This is an important point: You want the white paper to look attractive, but if it is too attractive, it will not be read.

This chapter will quickly touch on the key formatting elements of a white paper.

COVER PAGES

The traditional white paper includes a cover page. The core elements of a cover page include the white paper title, subtitle and date. Some white paper cover pages also include an author name, brief table of contents, an abstract and a copyright statement. Graphical treatments may also be added to a cover page to make it more attractive to the reader (see Figure 1).

Cover pages are becoming less common for white papers, especially shorter ones. The cover page can sometimes prevent a reader from diving into the white paper. If the layout or the few words on the cover page do not grab readers, they may never turn the page and begin reading your work.

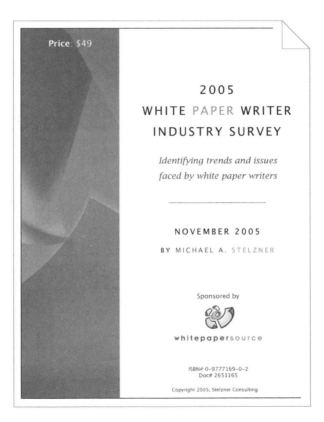

Figure 1: Sample cover page

The alternative to a cover page is to simply include your title and subtitle at the top of the first page of your document. Follow immediately with the opening paragraphs of your white paper. This is advantageous because readers will start reading the white paper in seconds and hopefully be lured deeper into your document.

ILLUSTRATIONS, CHARTS AND PHOTOS

Because white papers are very heavy on text, it makes good sense to try to break things up by adding some graphical elements. The most logical places to include graphics include the market drivers section and the places where you discuss your solution. In the market drivers portion of your white paper, you might include charts that show marketplace growth or diagrams that help convey market shifts. In the specific solution section of your white paper, screen shots and photographs of your product are very common.

Photographs can be used sparingly to enhance the story of your white paper. The history section of your white paper is an excellent place to include a photograph. Stock photography can be used to convey a key point. For example, if one of your problems is overworked call center staff, you could quickly locate royalty-free images of people on the phone at a call center. See Appendix III for a list of stock photography sources.

Process diagrams are very useful when discussing solutions (see Figure 2). At its most basic level, a simple diagram can be produced in PowerPoint or Visio and imported into Word or your desktop publishing application. Adobe Illustrator or Photoshop could be used to develop more advanced process diagrams. Ideally, a diagram should be developed by in-house designers or outsourced to professional illustrators.

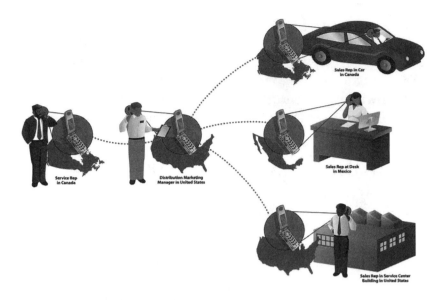

Figure 2: This process diagram was designed to demonstrate international push-to-talk technology.[1]

Another graphical element is the table. A simple table can break up the text in a white paper and help the reader quickly digest information. Tables are well-suited for benefits or "what to look for" lists.

SUBHEADS AND EXTRACTS

As a general rule of thumb with white papers, try to break large sections of content into smaller, easy-to-digest pieces. If you find a section is exceeding four paragraphs, it might make sense to break things down. The easiest way to accomplish this is with subheads. Because many readers are generally skimming white papers, subheads can help them quickly move through the white paper or keep them reading because they see the next section is only a few paragraphs away.

---

[1] Designed by Court Patton. See his other great work at http://www.pattonbros.com.

For example, if your white paper explores three key problems and the result is ten paragraphs of text, try breaking the content into subsections. Consider leading with a short introductory paragraph and then creating descriptive subheads for each problem.

Text extracts are another way to help readers travel through your white paper. By including a short descriptive sentence in the left margin or embedded in the text, it helps readers understand the section they are about to read or summarizes topics for readers skimming the document. When writing an extract, try to create an original sentence that paraphrases a section of your white paper, rather than copying words directly from your writing.

USING WHITE SPACE

White space is the area on the page where there is no text. With white papers, white space should be used generously. Many projects use a wide left margin of 2.5 inches, a 1.25-inch right margin and a 1-inch top and bottom margin. Text extracts are placed in the wide left margin, and the remaining white space enables readers to take notes when they print the white paper.

Adding bulleted lists also helps increase the use of white space. Some writers like to add an extra return after each bulleted item to create more space in a document.

Line spacing is another way to add more white space. Most white papers use single line spacing; however, 1.5 line spacing can help add more room to a white paper that needs a bit more length.

FOOTERS AND HEADERS

Most white papers include footers and headers. The first page header is usually distinct, and in some cases may include a document number and publication date.

Information residing in the footer and header depends on the needs of the company sponsoring the white paper. Typically, the header will include a company logo, the title of the white paper and the words "White Paper." If you have a long title, it is appropriate to abbreviate it in the header on subsequent pages beyond the first page.

The footer usually includes a page number, a copyright statement and a website address. Some white papers also add telephone numbers and document numbers.

COLUMNS

Most white papers are single-column documents. However, for a more formal, newspaper-type look, consider a two-column layout. Most word-processing software can easily accommodate two-column layouts, but the use of a wide left margin in a two-column design can be challenging based on the software's limitations. In addition, graphics often must be placed at the top or bottom of a two-column layout because of the text wrapping limitations.

DISTRIBUTION: PDF VERSUS PRINT

Once you have completed your white paper, you need decide if you want to print it professionally, distribute it exclusively as an electronic document or do both.

In the past, white papers were offset printed and distributed, similar to brochures. The document would be formatted, laid out in a professional desktop publishing application and sent to a printer. However, white papers often tend to be "living" documents, meaning they are regularly modified and updated as a market or product changes, making the offset printing process overly expensive.

Many businesses simply output white papers on laser printers and staple them together; a very acceptable practice for physical distribution with other product collateral.

However, the most common way of distributing white papers is simply as an electronic Adobe PDF document. Because most white papers are sent via e-mail or downloaded from the web, PDF files make perfect sense. In addition, PDF files retain formatting, are easily searchable and can be quickly printed, making them more valuable to the reader.

This chapter provided a brief overview of some white paper formatting tips. Once the paper is complete, you should come up with a marketing plan. The next chapter will introduce some of the many marketing methods available for white papers.

✳ Chapter 11 ✳

Marketing With White Papers

"Creative without strategy is called 'art.' Creative with strategy is called 'advertising'."

—Jef I. Richards

Worms and white papers share one thing in common—they're both effective bait. You don't fish in your bathtub; you cast into shady open waters. Likewise, to effectively capture leads with white papers, go where the prospects are. When a good white paper lands in front of the right person, it's a highly effective lead generation tool. To open a floodgate of leads with your white papers, they must be placed in front of potential customers.

This chapter's objective is to introduce ways to leverage your marketing arsenal's most compelling lures—your white papers—to generate qualified leads. If you are responsible for marketing your white paper, this chapter will be of particular interest to you. If you are not directly involved with marketing, read this chapter to help your company or client understand how the white paper can be used to best achieve its objectives. This chapter only provides an overview of some of the available options for marketing your white paper.

WHITE PAPER LEAD GENERATION CHALLENGES

Here are a few challenges that prevent many marketing professionals from fully leveraging a white paper's lead generation power:

Post and Hope

With an "if you build it, they will come" mentality, companies often put forth an enormous effort to produce a white paper, only to post it on their website among other marketing collateral, such as datasheets and case studies. There's nothing wrong with having white papers on the corporate website—after all, there's a high likelihood that after prospects jump through hoops to find your white paper, they will be interested in reading it.

However, white papers are akin to super-powered magnets that can easily attract leads outside the company website. To draw a visual picture, imagine fishing for tuna in only 2 feet of water. You might actually attract something near the shore, but big fish live in much deeper waters.

Your website is probably not one of the first places prospective customers visit when seeking solutions to their problems. Your white paper needs to be where the fish are. Rather than posting and hoping, savvy marketing professionals are turning to post-and-promote techniques.

Late Delivery

White papers are often used in the later stages of a sales cycle; perhaps as a "leave behind" after a client meeting. While white papers can help close existing prospects, they are also very effective for generating presales leads because executives and decision-makers rely on white papers when researching solutions to problems. Delivering a benefits-focused white paper to prospects doing research is a very effective form of marketing.

Poorly Crafted

A white paper is not a brochure, a datasheet or a product brief. One thing all these documents share in common is the assumption the reader has decided to make a purchase and is narrowing the analysis to feature comparisons. A white paper is typically used much earlier in the sales cycle and must be devoid of the language found in typical marketing collateral.

Symptoms of a poorly crafted white paper include immediate promotion of a product or service and a strong focus on features. This self-serving approach to writing white papers turns most readers off immediately.

WHITE PAPER SYNDICATION

A popular form of white paper advertising and lead generation involves promotional targeting of white papers via syndication networks. This type of white paper marketing commonly involves distributing your white paper through a network of specialty websites. With syndication services, you pay a service provider to place your white paper across a network of vertically oriented websites that are targeted based on your ideal lead. For a list of syndication companies, see Appendix III.

Key Considerations for Syndication Vendors

When seeking a source for white paper syndication and advertising, be sure to examine the following items:

Targeting ability: Seek a vendor that can target both your industry and your ideal reader. The vendor should delineate leads based on titles or job function; for example, a senior IT manager in the health services space or CIOs in mid-sized or larger corporations. Many vendors claim industry targeting but cannot refine leads to the job function level.

Breadth of properties: Look for a vendor that has partnerships with a wide range of content sites to increase the penetration of your white paper marketing efforts via multiple channels.

Lead support: Seek a solution that provides leads in a user-friendly format, such as a CSV file or an interface to CRM services, such as Salesforce.com.

Analysis: The ideal vendor should provide a comprehensive historical analysis that reveals how your white paper campaigns are performing.

QUALIFYING A WHITE PAPER SYNDICATION VENDOR

When looking for a place to syndicate your white paper, you need to shop wisely. The choices and services offered by white paper syndication outlets vary widely. Howard Sewell of ConnectDirect.com, a company that specializes in helping businesses generate leads with white papers, provides the following list of important questions to ask any syndication vendor.[1]

1. What's the demographic profile of the person downloading white papers from your site or network?

When choosing any advertising vehicle, the more detail you have on audience demographics, the more confident you can be that your white paper will be read by the right people. Most reputable vendors will readily supply statistics on job titles, company size, geography and more.

2. Is the contract price based on cost-per-lead or fixed price per period of time? What guarantees do I have on lead volume? What happens if you don't meet that minimum?

Increased competition in the white paper syndication market has resulted in a trend toward guaranteed

---

[1] This section is adapted from Sewell, H. (2005). *WhitePaperSource*. Ten tough questions to ask your white paper syndication vendor, http://www.whitepapersource.com/marketing/10questionsforsyndicators.html. Reprinted by permission of Howard J. Sewell.

performance. However, how the minimum performance is achieved and what happens when it is not vary greatly. Some vendors will launch additional e-mail, sponsorships, featured listings or other targeted promotions to increase your leads, while others may just keep your materials posted until the guarantee is met.

3. If there are guarantees, what constitutes a lead? For example, will I have to pay for consultants or students who download my paper?

Some media vendors count every lead toward your guarantee, no matter how qualified. If a measurable percentage of your leads are non-starters, your actual lead total can be much less and the cost-per-lead will be much higher than advertised.

4. What percentage of total downloads or traffic is international? Will I have to pay for international leads if I don't want them?

For many vendors, particularly the larger players with broad syndication networks, 50 percent or more of all traffic and leads can come from outside North America. This is great if you serve foreign markets. However, if you do not want such leads, your actual cost-per-lead could be double what the vendor is promising. Ask if there's a way to eliminate or not pay for leads from specific geographies.

5. Can you provide references?

It's easy for vendors to throw around performance numbers. However, sometimes the best evaluation of any site or network is a subjective one. Ask for references. Call those individuals and ask about the service they received, any problems they experienced and the quality of the delivered leads.

6. What's the typical lead volume for a white paper in my category?

Most providers won't be willing to give you actual lead numbers for specific white papers. Nevertheless, one way to get a good picture of overall performance is to ask for the total of all downloads per month across the network and the total number of white papers posted. The average downloads per white paper will paint a representative picture of the site's performance.

7. How do you drive traffic to your site or network?

Vendors use a variety of tools for driving traffic to their site, including e-mails to their registered user base, paid search advertising, placement on partner sites and banner ads. Ask the vendor what they do to bring in leads.

8. Do users receive alerts when new white papers are added? If so, how? How many registered users are there? What's the typical response to this alert?

Most advertisers see a big spike in downloads when their content first appears on the network, and user alerts are the reason why. The larger the registered user base, the better the response. Even better is a vendor who only sends relevant alerts to individual users who have expressed an explicit interest in your category of content.

9. What's the user experience on the site? How can I feel confident that someone searching for information will find my white paper?

Search procedures can be dramatically different from one site to the next. On some, content is easy to find. On others, it's buried beneath layers of other information. Don't judge a vendor on their sales collateral alone. Visit the site and search for information on your category. How hard is it to find relevant content? Can you search by keyword or must you browse by category? If you are restricted to a categorical listing, is there a category that matches up well with your product or service?

10. If I renew my contract, how will the pricing change from the initial agreement?

Renewal policies vary between vendors. Often, prices can change dramatically from one contract to the next and not just in the wrong direction. Some vendors offer renewing advertisers significant discounts. Either way, it's better to avoid surprises and gain a proper expectation up front.

LEADS VIA WEBSITE REGISTRATION

Posting a white paper on your website and requesting users register to gain access to your paper is another way to collect leads. However, much debate surrounds this strategy. Answering the question, "Should we require prospective customers to register for our white paper?" requires a bit of thought. The short answer is yes. The long answer is maybe.

The real question is why do you have a white paper in the first place? My guess is to generate interest in your product, solution or strategy, and ultimately produce a lead. If lead generation is your objective, it is important to take steps that convert interested parties into leads.

People opposed to registration claim it's a barrier to accessing the white paper. However, when done properly, the registration form is a filter that sifts and qualifies leads.

Most white papers are written to generate leads. If you cannot capture a potential lead, you are fully reliant on the strength of the paper to hold its own and get the phone ringing. Capturing leads also helps you determine who is reading your white paper and where they are coming from. When done correctly, people do not mind registering.

If you are simply posting the title of your white paper and then asking for registration, forgo the process. If you are providing a title and a paragraph abstract of the white paper, highly consider registration. If you actually format the first few pages in HTML, then most certainly ask for registration.

Let's take a cue from the world of computer game developers. New games build interest by providing access to the first few levels of the game in a free demo. The goal is to hook users with a sample that entices them to purchase the game. Similarly, white papers that require registration should include the first few pages of content so readers can determine if it is worthwhile to fill out a form to receive the entire paper.

Providing the full text of the first page or two increases the lead quality by assuring those who register are truly interested in the offer. If readers are exposed to enough valuable and relevant content, they'll be willing to trade personal information for access to the white paper. The result is a filter on leads. Those who are truly interested in your topic and have resonated with what they have read will be the ones providing lead information.

Consider the following case example from VistaPrint, a company that targets ultra-small business owners with print products.

> Mike Ewing, vice president of North American Acquisitions for VistaPrint, wanted to push the boundaries of standard marketing processes. He explained, "With this endeavor, we started out with the hypothesis: If you give people something of value, in exchange they are willing to be marketed to." For Ewing, a key goal was to maximize the number of registrations for the paper and achieve a return on investment in three months.

> The key of the initiative was to create and distribute the white paper from an altruistic approach. Rather than selling a product, VistaPrint wanted to give concrete tools to independent businesspeople to help them economically market their businesses. "With the campaign, we needed to move our standard marketing about buying printed products to permission-based, and offer value to those prospective customers who might not be ready to buy today," recalled Ewing.

> The title of the white paper, "Marketing Your Business on a Shoestring Budget: A Practical Guide to Success," was carefully crafted. A deliberate decision was made not to refer to the document as a white paper because the target reader was unfamiliar with the term.

The results were staggering. VistaPrint had more than 5,000 registrants in 60 days and more than 10% of these registrants converted into a sale.[2]

The VistaPrint example included the first page of content and then asked people for their name, e-mail address and the type of business they operated.

With a simple form, you can ask the right questions that determine if lead follow-up is appropriate. Also, be sure to provide enough content to enable a reader to determine if the paper is worthy of registration. The result will be a lead from someone who has expressed interest based on what they have seen thus far. With that lead, you can go about your ultimate goal of selling.

Developing Brand Equity With Registrations

Presenting a white paper on your website and cultivating leads involves a careful strategy. Below is a proven method to ensure more prospects turn into clients.

Provide the first pages free: Consider literally taking the title, subtitle and first page or two of your white paper and formatting it in HTML to appear as an article.

Place the registration form out of sight: Be sure to place the registration form after the first page and below the bottom of the screen, so the user must scroll to realize registration is needed. This assures that those who register have most likely read the content and found it useful enough to register, increasing the quality of the registrant via self-qualification.

---

[2] Hartsock, N. (December 2005). *WhitePaperSource*. Major online print company uses educational white paper to drive permission-based marketing, http://www.whitepapersource.com/marketing/casestudy-vistaprint.html.

Keep required questions to a minimum: Only require what is absolutely needed to cultivate the lead into a sale. The less required information, the more likely a person will register for the white paper. The basics include name and e-mail address. It is okay to ask for a phone number, but consider making it optional. Lastly, include a few questions with drop-down menus, such as, "How did you hear about us?" If you have a newsletter or want to build a list for a future newsletter, ask prospects if they would like to receive your newsletter as well. You could also ask if the reader would like further information on your topic with a simple yes or no question.[3]

Post a privacy statement: Be sure to include a privacy and spam statement, indicating you keep their personal information private and do not spam.

Explain how it will be sent: During the registration process, mention the white paper will be emailed. This will ensure the e-mail address entered is a legitimate address.

Provide quotes from readers: Include a few quotes that indicate how great the white paper is. This will encourage more people to register for the paper.

Send an automated e-mail: After the registrant answers your questions, immediately send an automated e-mail to the prospect, thanking the reader for his or her interest in your white paper. This can usually be handled by a web-based script. Do not immediately send the paper. Include a small statement about your services while prospects are waiting for the paper.

---

[3] Visit this page http://www.stelzner.com/regsample.html and scroll down to see a sample registration form.

Sample Auto Response E-mail Message

Hello, White Paper Enthusiast!

Thank you for your interest in the White Paper "How to Write a White Paper: A White Paper on White Papers" from Stelzner Consulting. We will be sending it to you shortly.

While you are waiting for the paper, check out our white paper forum, an interactive discussion board for all things related to white papers. You can post your questions there for immediate help. Visit the forum at http://www.whitepapersource.com/forum/.

The professional staff at Stelzner Consulting are capable white paper writers and have a proven track record. If you would like to view samples of our white papers, please visit http://www.stelzner.com/copy-whitepapers.html.

Best Regards,
Stelzner Consulting's Response System
http://www.stelzner.com

The thank-you page: Rather than providing immediate access to the white paper, display a page that thanks the prospect for registering. On this page, you can link to the many related services your company has to offer. Explain what e-mail address the paper will be sent from so folks can be sure to add it to their e-mail "white list."[4]

Delay sending the white paper: On a delay of 30 minutes to a few hours, send an e-mail with the actual

---

[4] For a sample, see http://www.stelzner.com/thankyou.html.

paper attached OR send a link to the download page. Be sure to mention the other services you offer in the e-mail or on the download page.

Never send another unsolicited message: Unless the prospect opted into your newsletter list or has agreed to be contacted, do not send him or her future emails. Do not assume prospects want to hear about new products and services. All it takes is a few angry people to blacklist your website and then many readers will not receive any of your emails.[5]

By following the above suggestions, you will increase the quality of your leads and improve the brand equity of your company. Leads will improve because they will be self-qualified. Brand equity will improve because you will be presenting your name multiple times to the reader: first on the registration page, then on the thank-you page, in the initial "thanks for registering" e-mail, in the final e-mail with the white paper and of course with the white paper itself. Rather than meeting the instant desire of the reader by simply linking to a PDF file, you are gaining credibility and value in the eyes of the reader and decreasing the chance they will forget you and your white paper.

DRIVING READERSHIP WITH PAY-PER-CLICK ADVERTISING

Pay-per-click advertising is an excellent way to assure your white paper is read by people who are looking for your solution. Rather than advertising your company, you can actually advertise a specific white paper. To better understand how pay-per-click advertising campaigns such as Google AdWords and Yahoo! Search Marketing can help drive white paper readership, I interviewed Andrew Goodman, author of *Winning Results with Google AdWords* and co-founder of the blog

---

[5] To learn more about e-mail blacklists, see http://www.imediaconnection.com/content/3276.asp.

Traffick.com. This interview was originally conducted for WhitePaperSource.com. It is so relevant and to the point that I included it in its original question-and-answer format.

Stelzner: How can pay-per-click ads help increase the readership of white papers?

Goodman: Pay-per-click campaigns can bring many targeted customers directly to a white paper. The beauty of pay-per-click ads that appear near search results is that they show up when someone may be in active research mode. If you intercept professionals early in their sales cycles, while they are still thinking about pertinent issues, you actually position yourself very well.

The process may be as simple as this: 5% of the people who see your ad on a term such as "semiconductor research" may find the ad relevant enough to click on it at a cost of, let's say, 25 cents per click. That click can go to a target page on your website. Perhaps 15% of those visitors to your website might then download your free white paper. The fact that a steady stream of prospects are reading your white paper and understanding your unique positioning sharply increases the chances you will gain customers.

Presumably, you may also seek permission to contact them further by asking them for their e-mail address in the download process. A relationship is initiated very inexpensively to a highly targeted prospect.

Stelzner: Why are pay-per-click ads valuable?

Goodman: Four keys include non-intrusiveness, pay only for interested prospects (clicks), extreme targeting (by keyword, and possibly even by region) and track-ability with fast feedback cycles.

Stelzner: Which pay-per-click ad service should technical audiences consider?

Goodman: Google AdWords is number one here because Google is the search engine of choice for technical audiences, at least as far as wide-reaching search tools go. Reach must be considered, even if you're in a niche. Many smaller ad networks may not generate any appreciable volume. The top pay-per-click services are always seeking out new partnerships and are trying out innovative content targeting models, so the terrain does keep changing.

Stelzner: What type of budgets should people consider for campaigns?

Goodman: If you are organizing your campaign properly, choosing the right keywords and phrases, writing prequalifying ad copy and bidding sensibly, then you want every click you can possibly generate. Every click should, on average, be a moneymaker for your business.

Some technical words can be very expensive, perhaps $10 or more per click, because three or four companies dominate a very small space and all are trying to grab the attention of their client base. Click volume will often be small in such cases, though. Largely, business-to-business and technical types of campaigns are less expensive than retail because of low volume, and yet may be much higher per click on some phrases. I've had cases where a client has "tried" to spend $1,000 per month. The volume just wasn't there and they could only spend $500.

Someone in a decision-making role does have to perform a search for your keywords, and if they don't, you don't spend. Sounds like small potatoes, maybe spending only a few hundred dollars a month, but last time I checked, marketing was supposed to be about making money, not spending it. Startups with generous marketing budgets may be able to spend substantially more by targeting a wider range of terms with the hopes of raising public awareness of a technology that few know exists. It depends on one's goals and on how one measures return on investment.

Stelzner: How should someone who is new to pay-per-click get started?

Goodman: Most pay-per-click services are meant to be self-service, but not everyone feels equally comfortable with the task of building and monitoring a campaign. It does make sense to outsource or seek a professional's help. In many cases, a third-party primer, such as my book, is an inexpensive way to get up to speed on the do's and don'ts.

In general, I'm a big advocate of going back to first principles or just reading mind-expanding material to get the creative juices going when it comes to understanding issues such as market differentiation and copywriting. Try books like *Survival Is Not Enough* by Seth Godin and *Net Words* by Nick Usborne. For fun, look at Michael Lewis' *Moneyball*. Reading articles at SearchEngineWatch.com is also a good idea to understand the whole context of online search and search marketing.

OTHER MARKETING IDEAS

If white papers are written well and targeted with precision, they should include highly desirable content that can generate excellent-quality leads. A few other ways to market with white papers include:

- As a call to action for an advertisement or direct mail piece
- Handing them out at trade shows
- Submitting them to a trade publication as contributed articles
- Sending copies to all of your customers
- Inserting them in company sales packets
- Hiring a public relations company to promote the paper and its underlying concepts

This chapter introduced a number of successful marketing tactics for white papers. Be sure to visit www.whitepapersource.com/marketing/ for white paper marketing articles and case studies. The appendixes following this chapter include many samples and valuable resources to help you improve your white paper.

Be sure to visit <u>www.writingwhitepapers.com</u> for more information about this book and other products and services that will help you capture readers and keep them engaged.

✳ Appendix I ✳

White Paper Quick Start Guide

This appendix was designed to help provide you a quick reference to the key first steps involved with writing any white paper.

Ten Steps for the Needs Assessment

1. Meet with key decision-makers.
2. Clearly identify the topic.
3. Discuss the ideal reader in detail.
4. Identify important secondary readers.
5. Establish the white paper's objective.
6. Create the outline.
7. Identify topical experts.
8. Set up expert interview times.
9. Determine the project completion date.
10. Gain approvals on the topic, ideal reader, objective and outline.

Key Questions to Ask About the Ideal Reader

- What are the person's title and job responsibilities?
- In what industry does this person work?

- What type of company does this person work for?
- How familiar is this reader with our topic?

Common White Paper Objectives

- **Generate sales leads**: This means the white paper is to be used early in the sales cycle and focused on business challenges and benefits.
- **Establish thought leadership**: This type of white paper is meant to demonstrate forward thinking and cement a company into a leadership position in the eyes of its readers.
- **Help close a sale**: This means the white paper will be used late in the sales cycle and will focus on technical details and processes.

Popular Outline Elements

- **Top problems or needs**: Addresses challenges faced by your ideal reader to build affinity.
- **Market drivers**: Discusses key industry trends to show change and persuade.
- **Historical overview**: Reviews how the market has evolved and is a transition toward the solution.
- **Generic solution definition**: Defines a company-agnostic product category where your product lives.
- **Benefits**: Reviews reasons the ideal reader should consider the solution.
- **The "what to look for" list**: Includes key considerations when examining a solution.
- **How it works**: Describes steps and processes to illustrate how the solution works.
- **Examples**: Includes hypothetical or actual case examples.

- **Specific solution advantages**: Explicitly describes your solution and its advantages.
- **Call to action**: Provides a compelling reason for a reader to take the next step.

Interviewing Tips

- Good questions ask "Why?"
- Great questions ask for three or four reasons or examples.
- Excellent questions ask about implications.
- When the answer to a question is short, ask your expert to elaborate or to describe things so a person unfamiliar with the topic can understand.

Writing the First Page

- Clearly identify the ideal reader.
- Briefly summarize the challenge.
- Very briefly introduce the solution.
- State the goal of the white paper.

❋ Appendix II ❋

White Paper Samples

SAMPLE 1: VERSERA WHITE PAPER

Owning It: How Personal Accountability Can Transform an Organization

For organizations that consistently struggle to meet goals or simply cannot pinpoint why things are not working as they should, worker accountability may be an issue that needs examination. Some clear symptoms of accountability deficiencies include blaming and finger-pointing, unclear and changing expectations, and difficulty retaining quality employees. When any or all of these issues are occurring within departments or across the organization, personal accountability levels need to be seriously investigated.

When employees take ownership of tasks and the action plan is clear, personal accountability emerges, lowering stress, increasing productivity, influencing job satisfaction and ultimately propelling the organization to its goals and beyond. This paper will examine the concept of personal accountability in the workplace and introduce some powerful techniques to bring employees to the point of saying "I'll own that!"

Why Personal Accountability?

In the 1940s, President Truman made famous the phrase "the buck stops here," in direct response to the popular expression "pass the buck." In his farewell presidential address, he said, "The president—whoever he is—has to decide. He can't pass the buck to anybody. No one else can do the deciding for him. That's his job."

Somewhere over the last 60 years, the concept of accountability has lost its popularity. Some attribute its fall to a culture of self-absorption, a feeling of entitlement or a moral decline. For example, in the late 1960s, the prevailing wisdom was that society, rather than the individual, was to blame for personal problems. No-fault divorce and no-fault auto insurance emerged.

In modern times, corporate executives, such as those at WorldCom and Enron, disowned responsibility for the criminal actions of their businesses. Often, executives are praised and given large exit bonuses for failing to do their jobs, sending a poor message to employees. It is passé in today's politically correct age to take responsibility and hold oneself accountable when things go wrong. To alter the course to "acceptable failure," businesses must reexamine their corporate culture and determine if they embrace passing the buck or taking ownership of the good, the bad and the ugly.

Destination "Acceptable Failure" by Way of Aimless Goals

When accountability and clarity are nowhere to be found, organizations can predictably determine the outcome of tasks: **failure**. Consider a story about four people named EVERYBODY, SOMEBODY, ANYBODY and NOBODY, who all work at the same company.

There was an important job to be done and EVERYBODY was sure that SOMEBODY would do it. ANYBODY could have done it, but NOBODY did it. Now SOMEBODY got angry because it was EVERYBODY's job. EVERYBODY thought ANYBODY could do it, but NOBODY realized that EVERYBODY would not do it. In the end, EVERYBODY blamed SOMEBODY when NOBODY did what ANYBODY could have done.

Had EVERYBODY agreed to a common goal and SOMEBODY volunteered to take ownership, ANYBODY would have been happy to help complete the task and the results would have been very different.

The Challenges of Poor Workforce Accountability

When everything is working well, accountability is understood and embraced in the corporate world. However, when problems emerge, excuses seem to be the acceptable alternative. The desire to embrace accountability during good times and run from it during bad times is the root of many problems in corporate America. However, to achieve success, employees must embrace personal accountability all the time.

Some of the most common signs that personal accountability is absent from the workplace include assigning blame to others, the prevalence of nebulous expectations and the inability to retain high achievers.

Blame and Finger-Pointing

When personal accountability is absent from the corporate culture, pinning the blame on others is one of the most common behaviors employees engage in when things go wrong. Do any of these charges sound familiar?

- "It's because of those strict regulations."
- "Our partner dropped the ball."
- "Sales just didn't close deals."
- "Jack in Receiving was slacking off."

Blame and finger-pointing stem from workplace anxiety, conflict, distrust and confusion. In this type of environment, employees talk about—rather than to—each other. Typically, the informal meetings that occur after meetings, also known as hallway discussions, are where real opinions are heard.

When being held accountable leads to demotion or job loss, employees will refrain from accepting responsibility for the outcomes of their work. If the boss does not model accountability, blame and finger-pointing will be the norm for his or her employees.

When something goes wrong with an **accountable** employee, he or she will say, "This is what I did. This is what I learned from my mistake. This is how I will change, and I accept responsibility."

Unclear and Changing Expectations

When managers lack personal accountability, they are often unclear with their expectations or routinely change objectives, resulting in confusion and incomplete goals. Consider these sample expectations:

- "Diversity is very important and we will embrace it."
- "We will change our IT systems to keep up with the times."
- "We will focus on innovation this year."

Because there is no depth behind these expectations, goals will be too vague and the end game will remain unclear. Without any kind of clarity, the outcome of these types of expectations is no outcome at all.

Employees want to know what road to travel, the tasks they need to accomplish and milestones along the way. However, when expectations are changing or unclear, it is akin to running a race with no clear finish line. The result will be burnout, lack of motivation and purposeless effort.

Ideally, to hold employees accountable, tasks must be clearly defined up front, the expected outcomes must be explained and all parties must agree upon actionable steps.

Difficulty Retaining Quality Employees

Often a lack of accountability leads to equal rewards for unequal efforts among employees, spurring the best workers to see no value in working hard to further the goals of the business. High achievers will ultimately leave organizations that do not hold employees accountable.

For example, consider two sales teams. One exceeds its goals and the other does not. However, the company assigns bonuses based on total sales of both teams combined. Because one team worked hard, the other team received its bonus without earning it. This approach ends up rewarding those who do not deserve reward. Whether salespeople perform or not, they still get their bonuses. When a lack of measurement exists, high achievers will not prosper.

When people are accountable, they are more productive; some estimates say twice as productive and more satisfied. To retain high achievers, everyone must be held accountable for their actions.

Other Challenges

Additional symptoms that point to a lack of accountability include:

- Poor meeting management
- Overuse of "we" and underuse of "I"
- Indirect and unclear communication

- Hindered creativity
- Gossip
- Conflict

Steps to Achieving Personal Accountability

Helping employees accept personal accountability for tasks is a multi-step process that begins with workers taking full ownership of a task and its outcome at the time the task is assigned. Employees must have a preexisting mindset that they can and will get tasks accomplished.

Once employees are willing to take responsibility, a clear agreement must be in place between the task assigner and the task owner. The agreement must clearly articulate the task, the expected results and when it must be completed.

After employees are willing to take responsibility and agree on what will be produced, they must be willing to take personal action to see that results occur.

Finally, employees must be willing to answer for outcomes, whether good or bad. When all of these steps are in place and employees have committed to them, personal accountability will emerge.

1 PERSONAL RESPONSIBILITY
A preexisting mindset of personal ownership and commitment to a task

2 CLEAR AGREEMENT
Who owns task, what are the agreed-upon results, what is the deadline

3 PERSONAL EMPOWERMENT
Taking personal action to ensure results are achieved

4 PERSONAL ACCOUNTABILITY
A personal willingness to answer for outcomes, good or bad

The Benefits of Accountable Employees

When employees embrace personal accountability, the following benefits occur:

- Personal action is taken to overcome obstacles and ensure results are achieved
- Results are on target because the task, owner, expected results and deadline are clear
- Individuals display a willingness to answer for the results of their actions
- Productivity increases because employees, teams and entire departments are more effective and individuals agree to own tasks
- Job satisfaction improves because tasks are clearly defined, success occurs more often and individuals are encouraged to take on new tasks
- Negative events become learning events
- Blaming and finger-pointing are reduced
- Workarounds and project restarts are significantly reduced
- Employees are more likely to ask for clarification

Personal Accountability Training: Convincing Employees to Embrace Accountability

Instilling personal accountability into a corporate culture is critical for organizations that want to maximize results and retain quality employees. Personal accountability training is targeted at leaders, management and the general workforce. Shifting the mindset of the culture is no simple task, but the benefits to the organization are significant. Comprehensive personal accountability training is the best way to encourage employees to take ownership of and responsibility for tasks.

The purpose of personal accountability training is to help employees understand the importance of accountability, identify why the organization values accountable employees, discuss each individual's role in the process and encourage employees to reexamine their attitudes and actions. The result often shifts an employee's frame of mind to accept personal empowerment, responsibility and accountability.

Personal accountability training usually begins with a comprehensive self-assessment of an individual's disposition toward being accountable, as well as an assessment of departmental or organizational attitudes towards accountability. An interactive workshop walks employees through a process that reveals accountable and unaccountable behaviors and actions, defines accountability, discusses why it is important and provides guidance on how to make the concept part of employees' jobs. In addition, case studies, small-group discussions and application situations guide the learning process. A post-training assessment helps determine if the corporate culture is shifting to accept responsibility and accountability.

Accountability in Action: Corporate Example

Accountability training affects even the simplest tasks within an organization. Consider the annual performance review process:

Unaccountable Organization

Ann is a manager scheduled to conduct an annual performance review with her employee, John. She is reasonably sure that John thinks he is getting a good review; however, Ann is disappointed with John's performance. He lacks initiative and problem-solving skills and is unwilling to do anything he thinks is outside of his job description. John takes great pride in the fact that what he does do is done perfectly, but he takes too long on things that do not need to be perfect. Many of John's coworkers are frustrated with him and routinely complain to others about him.

When the review day comes, Ann expresses dissatisfaction and tells John he is not motivated. John is hurt and acts defensive, eventually becoming uncommunicative. Ann tells John that she is only giving him half of the normal raise and will review his situation again in six months.

Following the review, John mopes around. There is no real change in his work behavior, but he continues to handle his basic responsibilities. Ann continues to be unhappy with John's lack of initiative and responsiveness, but when six months is up, she approves the rest of his raise.

Accountable Organization

In an organization with a culture of accountability, John's behavior would not be supported or rewarded. Ann would not wait until the annual review to tell John that he is not performing to the expectations she and the organization have for him.

Ann would be meeting with John regularly to make sure he is clear on what he should be doing, when assignments should be done and what the results should be. She would make clear agreements with John about when and how he should take initiative and would address his lack of problem-solving skills. Should John fail to deliver on agreements, he would be asked to identify what he could do better next time. Co-workers would be talking to John about their frustrations, instead of talking about him to others.

John would understand that his inability to get the full raise he was eligible for was ultimately his responsibility and he would own the fact that he was underperforming. John would actively seek clarification from Ann and others about what he could do better and would make a concerted effort to improve.

What to Look for in an Accountability Training Provider

When seeking a company to aid in the process of teaching employees to embrace personal accountability, many factors should be considered, including:

Bias towards participant accountability: Seek a program that empowers and holds participants accountable to transfer accountability skills back into the workplace. Rather than treating employees as empty vessels that need to be filled with accountability knowledge, a good program should ensure participants walk away with skills that can be applied and later tested to ensure they were retained.

Seeks to alter behaviors and improve skills: Look for a program that not only reveals existing behaviors that undermine accountability, but also helps to build a foundation for improving accountability skills and altering counterproductive behavior. The teaching program should adopt a holistic process that leverages advanced learning activities and follow-up support, rather than a basic one-day crash course.

Delivers measurable results: A good program will include methodologies for analyzing the impact of the training by examining the time spent in meetings, the percentage of projects completed on time, the reduction of false starts as a result of clear up front agreements and decreased employee turnover.

Offers an individual assessment: Look for a program that assesses the accountability attributes and behaviors of each participant to identify areas where employees can improve.

Incorporates a high level of interactivity: Seek a program that uses small-group interaction, sharing experiences and group activities to ensure greater learning retention.

Includes video modeling: A good accountability training program will include actors modeling poor and proper communication methods via video. Video modeling intensifies learning by demonstrating counterproductive actions in a nonthreatening manner.

Prepares trainers to be internal agents of change: An effective program must train existing employees to teach accountability training and hold employees accountable.

Utilizes proven instructional methods: Be sure the program includes a blend of proven, research-based learning methods.

The provider is accountable: Work with a training company that holds itself accountable for results by measuring behavior and knowledge changes, ensuring a more powerful bottom-line impact on the company. The training company should also deliver on its promises, meet commitments and be able to verify results.

Versera Performance Learning's Accountability Training Program

Designed to create a culture of change where employees take responsibility for tasks and answer for good and bad results, Versera Performance Learning's accountability training program offers a comprehensive approach to altering the corpo rate culture to embrace accountability. Designed to teach every employee in a department or organization to own tasks and accept responsibility, the program helps instill empowerment and accountability.

The program begins with a four-day "train the trainer" experience, where key employees are taught to deliver the program to exacting standards that will generate results. The main program includes an assessment of each participant's skills and attitudes toward accountability concepts, a one-day interactive training workshop and post-program follow-up.

The accountability training program includes:

- Written case studies
- A scripted leaders' guide
- Discussion questions
- Group activities
- Participant workbooks
- Presentation materials
- Videos that model behavior
- An accountability assessment

- Built-in metrics
- Online follow-up tools and resources

Program Advantages

Versera Performance Learning's accountability program meets all of the requirements outlined in this paper. A few key advantages include:

Proven learning model: Versera Performance Learning's accountability training program is built on a unique, yet proven, learning model that not only teaches accountability concepts, but alters participants' mindsets. Employees come to grasp that accountability starts with them owning what they will take away from the training and puts a successful outcome squarely on their shoulders.

Goes beyond training: Versera Performance Learning's accountability training program is not simply a training event, it is a process. Participants begin with discovery of their accountability skills and behaviors and proceed to learn and apply new behaviors. Finally, each employee is analyzed after the training to see if change has occurred.

Results-oriented: Versera Performance Learning is committed to delivering results and has designed methods for measuring accountability learning and the degree to which learning has been transferred to the workplace. Measurements are easy to implement and do not require an expert to interpret results.

About Versera Performance Learning

To find out more about Versera Performance Learning, visit www.verseralearning.com or call 1-877-958-8300.

SAMPLE 2: ONE TOUCH GLOBAL TECHNOLOGIES WHITE PAPER

Instantly Connecting Documents with Workers

Integrating Business Process Workflow Into a Document Management System

Information is the lifeblood of corporations. When purchase orders, invoices, credit applications, expense reports, and medical and insurance claims are addressed quickly, businesses succeed. However, when the management and distribution of documents and business information falters, data is lost, processes are incomplete, progress slows and compliance concerns emerge.

How can CIOs and IT managers ensure the right information quickly flows to critical workers and that proper measures are taken? Fortunately, advanced document management solutions exist that integrate business process workflow and ensure important printed and electronic information is retained, searchable and integrated into existing enterprise systems. The result is a highly efficient information procedure that automates employee processes and improves response times to customers, vendors and auditors.

This white paper will review emerging trends in information management and examine the benefits of integrating business process workflow into a document management system.

Market Drivers Impacting Information Management

Government regulations, the continued growth of data and inefficient workers are a few of the drivers encouraging IT to reexamine its information management practices.

Regulatory compliance has motivated businesses to organize their information. Companies in the financial, healthcare and insurance industries, as well as all publicly held businesses, are impacted by a wide variety of regulations that involve retaining key documents and securing information. When responding to an audit, businesses must be able to quickly recover relevant data, regardless of its format or location.

The amazing growth of business information is another market driver. According to Osterman Research, e-mail volume is growing between 35 and 40 percent annually.[1] IDC found that an average business will increase its data storage requirements by 40 to 50 percent in the next year alone, due largely to unstructured data.[2]

Improving the operational efficiency of workers has also become a major concern for IT. For example, knowledge workers spend an enormous amount of time seeking content that is often never found. An extensive study by IDC revealed that knowledge workers spend more than 27 hours a week searching, gathering and analyzing information.[3] The study also discovered that these employees spend 3.5 hours weekly searching for information that is never found and 3 hours a week recreating content. The report claims that automating repetitive steps and eliminating tasks that waste time will increase worker productivity and could save organizations millions of dollars.

Regulatory burdens, massive data growth and knowledge worker inefficiencies create a number of critical information challenges.

The Challenges of Information Mismanagement

There are three primary challenges associated with the improper management of documents and business information: lost data, inefficient processes and noncompliance.

Lost Information

Misplacing information is a common occurrence. This is especially true for businesses that handle paper. Whether

---

[1] Cook, R. (November 2004). *The Chief Executive*. Electronic dilemma: The e-mail explosion poses tricky challenges to CEOs, http://www.allbusiness.com/periodicals/article/253773-1.html.

[2] DuBois, L. (November 2005). Viewpoint: Unstructured Data Classification Mitigates Compliance and Security Risks, http://www.idc.com/getdoc.jsp?containerId=VWP000260.

[3] Feldmen, S., et al. (March 2005). The hidden costs of information work, http://www.idc.com/getdoc.jsp?containerId=201334.

documents are medical claims, mortgage applications, trade orders, credit applications or expense reports, paper has a way of getting lost. Even if information is recorded in electronic formats, such as in spreadsheets and Microsoft Word files, data can be easily forever misplaced.

People are bottlenecks. Because paper and documents lack the inherent ability to be tracked and audited, they often end up on someone's desk or in a spam folder. When a document has a critical path it must follow, it is important to know where it is, how it has been acted on and where it needs to go next.

When information is temporarily or permanently lost, a number of business implications emerge, including:

- Lost opportunities
- Liability issues
- Slower productivity
- Reduced customer satisfaction
- Compliance violations

In her 1997 book *Intranet Document Management,* Joann Bannan explained, "When confronted with the thousands of written works created by a medium-to-large business in the course of one day, too often we lose track of critical information with future value. Lost because you can't find it but it's still around 'somewhere.' Or permanently lost/deleted in the fury of cleaning a full e-mail box, or lost when the only person who knew where it was leaves the company. Does the future usefulness of someone's work have to depend on the successor?"[4]

Process Inefficiencies

Information constantly flows in and out of businesses. When customers, vendors, suppliers and prospects lack important documents, the relationship suffers.

When document processes are people-centric, they lead to human error, excess labor burden and opportunity loss. For example, consider a disconnect in the information workflow for a healthcare clinic that needs to fax a medical record to a hospital for a procedure. The document must be located, faxed,

---

[4] Bannan, J. (1997). *Intranet Document Management: A Guide for Webmasters and Content Providers.* Boston: Addison-Wesley.

routed and received in a timely manner. If the document is lost somewhere along its chain, the process must begin again, a costly process for workers and a burden on patients. Thus, slow processes drive up costs because of their manual labor requirements and limit a business's competitive ability.

Furthermore, the cost of doing business with paper in particular is very high. Documents must be copied, stored in expensive physical locations and easily retrieved and delivered. If a process takes too long, companies can lose business or be fined for being noncompliant. If documents are at the center of processes, it is critical to keep them in a central repository for easy reference.

Compliance Issues

Poor information retention and responsiveness to inquiries can expose a business to legal problems, regulatory fines and negative PR. Nearly all businesses are impacted by regulations such as Sarbanes-Oxley, Gramm-Leach-Bliley, OSHA (Occupational Safety and Health Act), HIPAA and IRS requirements. Financial services, health care and government agencies have additional compliance requirements.

Most regulations focus on the retention and security of records, regardless of whether the information resides on paper or in electronic formats, such as e-mail. Businesses need to know where information is, who has accessed it, if it is secured and how it can be recovered. Some regulations, such as those in the insurance industry, require that documents be acted on within a specified time to avoid penalties.

When a business does not know where information is and how it has been handled, and if it fails to generate a complete "production of documents," it cannot prove it has been compliant. The burden of proof rests on the business. If documents are not centralized and traceable, it is very costly to respond to a regulatory audit.

What is needed is a document management system that integrates with business process workflow to help organizations locate documents and track their progression through the documents' lifecycle.

A Brief History of Document Management

Prior to the mid-1990s, businesses were littered with paper documents in the forms of memos, faxes, letters, applications and hand-written notes. These documents lived in in-boxes,

**Not long ago, document management involved rows
of storage cabinets**

filing cabinets and storage rooms. With the wide-scale adoption of the Internet came the addition of e-mail and web-based content.

By the late 1990s, computing power increased significantly, operating systems became more flexible and technologies such as optical character recognition (OCR), optical markup recognition (OMR) and forms processing matured. The combination of these advancements allowed faxed or scanned documents to be transformed into searchable electronic files.

Document management systems provided a classification and identity system that tagged documents with important information, such as when a document was created, who authored it and its purpose.

Today's Document Management Challenges

Today's document management challenges are primarily related to accessibility, usability and security. Organizations are continually bombarded with more paper and information in a wide variety of formats. Businesses often lack a strategy to access documents in real-time. In addition, document management systems are being viewed as a convergence point for all information, but few have the ability to ensure information convergence is efficient and successful.

New solutions enable all content to be converged into electronic systems that enable clients, vendors and employees to efficiently act on information. However, content must also be extended to business intelligence systems, such as customer relationship applications and enterprise resource planning systems.

As more documents are integrated and automatically delivered to knowledge workers, companies will begin to see incredible efficiency improvements, be able to handle the growing deluge of data and quickly respond to audits without heavy burdens on the business.

The Solution: Integrating Business Process Workflow Into a Document Management System

To overcome the challenges of lost data, inefficient procedures and regulatory compliance, businesses are turning to document management systems that extend documents and business information into existing processes.

At their core, mature document management systems capture and store electronic and scanned paper documents into a centralized system that allows documents to be easily recovered, manipulated and acted upon. Documents may include Microsoft Word files, Acrobat PDF's, spreadsheets, faxes, e-mail, images, audio and video.

With document management, organizations can improve the creation, version control and storage of different documents within departments and across the company. Business rules and workflow automation can also be added.

If a document resides in a document management system, its data can be easily integrated into existing business processes. For example, accounts payable, accounts receivable, human resources, operations and other departments can easily act on documents when they need to be dealt with, without any manual effort. Business intelligence systems such as enterprise resource planning and customer relationship management can also seamlessly integrate content from document management systems.

Technologies employed include OCR, OMR, forms processing and barcode scanning. Text processing tools also define elements within a document that should be designated as important business content. Document output management can be used to update databases and generate new documents, e-mail, faxes, postal mail, EDI and XML transactions without manual intervention.

With business process workflows integrated into a document management system, organizations can improve the creation, collaboration, review, approval and management of content as it travels throughout the organization.

Important Benefits

A number of significant benefits emerge when business process workflows arc linked to document management systems, including:

Eliminating lost data: When a document is captured and tracked electronically, it can always be recovered, no matter where it is in its lifecycle. As a result, the misfiling of documents is drastically reduced or eliminated. In addition, each document automatically records who generated it, when it was created, who received it and how it was acted on. Now documents simultaneously arrive at the desks of the right people, in the right format and at the right time. This helps standardize processes and creates greater accountability for knowledge workers. In addition, the opportunity for human error is greatly reduced.

Improving process efficiency: Document management shortens the time needed to retrieve and act on critical information, improving knowledge worker productivity. For example, if a business is processing claims, a document management system that integrates workflow can reveal exactly where the claim is in its lifecycle, speeding the flow of information and eliminating backlogs. Predefined business rules can be automatically applied to a document to enforce processes, route the document and aggregate information from multiple documents, offloading knowledge workers. Now information and documents are immediately available and acted on, decreasing steps and accelerating turn-around. When information is readily available to knowledge workers, they are able to provide better customer service and more effectively perform other tasks. In addition, businesses can increase their profitability by cutting research time.

Aiding with compliance: With a document management system, all documents and information content can be easily searched and retrieved to produce a set of records in response to an audit. Now businesses can prove they are compliant with minimal effort and disruption to the business, dramatically reducing the cost of responding to an audit. In addition, automated processes help ensure businesses remain complaint by

controlling access to information, monitoring and reporting violations, and securely retaining or destroying documents.
    Other benefits include:

* Enables employee, partner and customer collaboration
* Securely stores content
* Reduces the cost of paper processing, paper storage, printing and distribution
* Provides a common environment for managing a wide range of documents and content
* Allows library-type services, such as checking documents in and out
* Cuts manual data entry tasks, significantly reducing order processing times and incorrect shipments

What to Look for in a Solution Provider

When looking for a company to integrate business process management into a document management system, be sure to consider the following requirements:
    Handles all types of content: Seek a solution that can accommodate all the different types of physical and electronic documents and information your business relies on, including e-mail, database entries, faxes, scanned documents and common document formats, such as Microsoft Word and Excel.
    Allows pre- and post-document processing: The right solution should process information as it arrives into the system and automatically trigger the appropriate actions based on the document's content, greatly speeding the decision-making process.
    Minimal impact on existing systems: Seek a solution that can be implemented with minimal retooling or modification of existing systems, reducing the need to alter workflow processes or abandon previous investments.
    System integration expertise: To help minimize the impact of a solution, look for a company that specializes in integrating document management into existing business intelligence systems.
    Built on the .NET platform: Look for a solution that leverages the Microsoft .NET platform when possible, and predefined workflow tools for systems such as SharePoint, BizTalk, Exchange, SQL Server and service oriented architectures for faster deployment and maximum flexibility.
    Automates procedures: The ideal solution should automate many formerly manual processes, including notification, fax-

backs and database entries. In addition, it should be easy to set up rules that trigger actions and repurpose information.

Extensive support: Try to find a company that will partner with you for the long-term. The company should provide consulting, implementation, training and support. Look for on-site and remote service packages.

Many strategic relationships: Work with a provider that understands the full range of available document management and automation technology, and can offer the best mix of products to meet the information needs of your business.

At least 10 years market experience: Seek a company that has been working with electronic document automation for at least 10 years, has a variety of customers and extensive market knowledge.

The One Touch Global Advantage

One Touch Global's name means accomplishing tasks with a single touch. Founded in 1991, the company is a provider of premier document management and workflow automation solutions including network fax, messaging, data capture, document imaging, business process automation, document output management, production scanning and archiving systems. As a Platinum systems integrator and Microsoft Certified Partner, One Touch Global specializes in the design and deployment of advanced information management solutions.

One Touch Global provides the following unique advantages:

- **Consulting**: One Touch Global will work within your existing processes to understand what you are doing and who is involved with the lifecycle of documents, keeping your organizational objectives in mind.
- **Systems integration**: One Touch Global helps business handle the entire lifecycle of documents via needs analysis, strategic planning, implementation, training and ongoing support.
- **Remote and on-site service**: Both on-site and remote services are available to enable troubleshooting in as little as 15 minutes.
- **More than 15 years experience**: One Touch Global understands document management and automation technology.
- **Extensive client base**: With a proven client base, One Touch Global can be trusted with your information

management implementations. A sampling of clients include Toshiba, New Century Mortgage, First Allied Securities, Primary Provider Management Company, American Family Insurance, Compartners Healthcare, Conseco Insurance, Club Med and Cal Spas.

To begin the first step toward controlling your documents, please call 1-800-233-3619 or e-mail eSales@otgt.com.

❋ Appendix III ❋

White Paper Resources

The following resources will be helpful guideposts for different stages of your white paper writing and marketing processes.

Top Resources

WhitePaperSource Newsletter: This is the first and leading electronic publication for white paper–related news, writing and marketing information. With more than 20,000 readers, the *WhitePaperSource Newsletter* includes content-rich articles, expert interviews, case studies and reviews. Be sure to sign up at whitepapersource.com/newsletter/.

White Paper Writer Industry Survey: The *White Paper Writer Industry Survey* is an annual survey of hundreds of white paper writers. The results focus on how white papers are written, formatted, distributed, structured and billed. See whitepapersource.com/report/.

White Paper Discussion Forum: If you have questions or want to explore some ideas with the world's leading experts on white papers, be sure to check out the WhitePaperSource Forum at whitepapersource.com/forum/.

White Paper Mentoring: If you are in need of professionals to help you through the process of producing a white paper, shepherding services are available that provide you direct access to white paper writing experts. For details, e-mail mentor@writingwhitepapers.com.

White Paper Training: If you have writers or professionals who need formal training on the process of writing white papers, a number of different options are available to train your staff. For more information, send an e-mail to training@writingwhitepapers.com.

Peer Reviewers

Are you looking for a professional to examine your white paper and provide suggested improvements? Peer reviews are helpful for writers who want sanity checks performed on their white papers. A small investment in a peer review service could make a big difference in the quality of your finished paper.

Michael Stelzner: I will review your existing white paper and provide extensive commentary on how to improve it. The peer review includes an assessment of your ideal reader, a detailed examination of the strength of your white paper and commentary on how to improve your document. For details, e-mail peerreview@writingwhite papers.com.

Gordon Graham: Graham, a seasoned technology white paper writer, can diagnose your white paper and prescribe how to clear up what ails it. He'll provide a detailed report, a frank analysis of your paper's strengths and weaknesses, and his personal prescription for how to get your white paper back on its feet. E-mail him at Gordon@ThatWhitePaperGuy.com.

Professional Organizations

While there is no professional organization that specializes in the craft of creating white papers, there are a few associations that are helpful for those seeking the advice of other writers.

Society for Technical Communication: For specialists in technical communication, this organization and its more than 18,000 members are an excellent resource. Membership options include local chapter involvement, *Intercom* magazine, *Technical Communication* journal, special-interest groups, forums and discussion groups, and a national convention. For more information, visit stc.org.

International Association of Business Communicators: This organization includes more than 13,000 business communication professionals. It has excellent resources, including its *Communication World* magazine. For more information, visit iabc.com.

Writing Standards

APA Style Guide: The APA citation style is an industry standard. For information on *The Publication Manual of the American Psychological Association*, visit apastyle.org.

MLA Style Guide: The Modern Language Association publishes a style guide that is commonly used in research papers, a close parallel to white papers. For information on the *MLA Handbook for Writers of Research Papers*, visit mla.org/publications.

Chicago Manual of Style: Another common style book is the *Chicago Manual of Style*. To learn more about it, visit chicagomanualofstyle.org.

Citing electronic documents: For a great discussion of how to cite websites, emails, forum posts and other electronic data sources via MLA, APA or the *Chicago Manual of Style*, see bedfordstmartins.com/online/citex.html.

Editors

Editorial and Production Services: If you are looking for a great white paper editor, contact Lisa Hernandez at edproserv@aol.com. She has been my editor for years and does excellent work.

Editorial Services Directory: For a directory of free-lance editors who belong to the Society for Editors, see editorsnsw.com/esd/.

Editors Association of Canada: If you are looking for editors based out of Canada, be sure to visit editors.ca.

Stylewriter: Stylewriter is a Windows-based software editor that applies more than 50,000 rules to your writing. If you cannot afford an editor, this may be the way to go. See editorsoftware.com.

Bullfighter: This free software will detect overused jargon in your writing. See fightthebull.com/bullfighter.asp.

Research

Google.com: The king of Internet search engines, Google is one of the first places to look for information on nearly any topic. Be sure to examine Chapter 5 for tips on using Google.

Yahoo.com: If you are coming up short on Google, give Yahoo a try.

ClickZ Stats: Looking for the latest trends in Internet research? ClickZ Stats (formerly CyberAtlas) offers extensive free research ranging from online revenues to global Internet usage. See clickz.com/stats/.

FindArticles.com: This is one of the largest repositories of magazine articles on the web and includes academic publications. Its many thousands of sources contain articles dating back to the 1980s. Some articles are free and others cost a fee to access.

KeepMedia.com: For writers looking for quick access to industry articles that cover 200 major publications, be sure to check out this resource. Portions of articles are provided and you must be a paid subscriber to access the rest. However, you can find information quickly with this resource.

MagPortal.com: This site is a simple and free search engine for searching magazine articles.

Finding Famous Quotes: If you are looking to add a creative flair to your writing, be sure to check out quotationspage.com, a site that allows you to search for famous quotes by author or subject.

Webopedia.com: Webopedia is an online dictionary for words, phrases and abbreviations that are related to computer and Internet technology.

Whatis.com: This site is another information-technology–focused encyclopedia that is good for defining acronyms.

Dictionary.com: When Microsoft Word does not recognize a word or its thesaurus is just too rudimentary, consider Dictionary.com, an excellent resource for spelling, word definitions and extensive synonyms.

Wikipedia.org: Known as the "Free encyclopedia anyone can edit," Wikipedia is an excellent resource with millions of articles that are refined by literally thousands of volunteers.

Federal Statistics: A great resource for finding U.S. Government statistics is located at fedstats.gov.

Almanac: If you are looking for an almanac, be sure to check out infoplease.com/almanacs.html.

Glossaries: For a searchable directory of hundreds of glossaries, take a look at glossarist.com.

Page Layout

Microsoft Word: The standard application used for writing white papers, Microsoft Word offers a comprehensive dictionary, spell checker, thesaurus, grammar checker, markup tools and basic layout capabilities. See Microsoft.com.

QuarkXPress: A powerful desktop publishing application and the choice for many graphic designers, QuarkXPress provides amazing design control to enhance the look and feel of your white paper. See quark.com.

Adobe InDesign: A newer player to the desktop publishing world, InDesign is an excellent tool that can import your Word documents and create attractive layouts. See Adobe.com.

Adobe Acrobat: This program creates Adobe PDF files, the international standard for distributing electronic documents. PDF files retain all of the look and feel of your original white paper document while enabling powerful search and markup capabilities. See Adobe.com.

Charting and Diagram Programs

ChartSmith: This excellent program makes very attractive 3D charts and diagrams. However, it is only available for the Mac. See blacksmith.com.

Microsoft Excel: This spreadsheet application can create a wide variety of pie charts, bar charts and just about any other diagram you would ever need. See Microsoft.com.

Microsoft Visio: For creating complex network diagrams, Visio is an excellent resource. See Microsoft.com.

Illustrators

Court Patton: For an excellent technical illustrator, be sure to call on Court Patton of Patton Brothers. He specializes in product illustrations, diagrams, process charts and any other technical illustrations. See pattonbros.com or call 619-463-4562.

Association of Illustrators: If you want to examine different illustration styles, the Association of Illustrators has online portfolios to help you find just the right artist. See theaoi.com/portfolios/.

Folioplanet.com: This site includes hundreds of online portfolios of illustrators and an artist finder that allows you to search by type of illustration.

Images and Photography

iStockphoto.com: This site is a very large and very reasonably priced source for excellent royalty-free photographs and illustrations. Prices start at $1 per image! You can also locate the original artist or photographer for custom work.

GettyImages.com: This is the world's largest source of stock photography for rights-managed and royalty-free images. Its collections are huge, the quality is excellent and the pricing is rather expensive. Expect to pay upwards of $200 for a single royalty-free image.

Corbis.com: This site is another excellent, yet smaller, collection of rights-managed and royalty-free images. Prices are more reasonable than Getty.

Recommended Books

White Paper Marketing Handbook: Robert W. Bly's *White Paper Marketing Handbook* is a great resource for helping businesses understand the value of educational marketing.

Copywriting That Sells High Tech: Janice King's book, *Copywriting That Sells High Tech* provides valuable insights and practical advice on writing clear and compelling promotional materials for technology products and services.

Informational Sites

WhitePaperSource.com: This site includes detailed articles on writing and marketing white papers, an active forum, industry news and many other white paper–related resources.

MarketingSherpa.com: MarketingSherpa is a unique site that specializes in news and case studies related to the business-to-business marketing world. White papers are regularly discussed in their articles. Be sure to subscribe to their newsletters.

MarketingProfs.com: This site is comprised of mostly contributed articles related to the general topic of marketing. However, there are numerous white paper–specific articles on the site.

SoftwareCEO.com: Although targeted at the software chief executive, this site has a lot of useful marketing information, including a marketing forum.

White Paper Repositories and Syndication Sites

Bitpipe.com: This technology-focused white paper site is one of the first and largest white paper repositories on the Internet. Owned by TechTarget, the site integrates with its publications such as *CIO Decisions* and *Information Storage*. This site only accepts fee-based white paper placement.

KnowledgeStorm.com: This site is a major white paper repository for technology-related white papers. KnowledgeStorm also has extensive syndication relationships with major publications such as *BusinessWeek*, *InfoWorld* and *Government Computer News*. White papers can be placed on this site and syndicated for a fee.

ITPapers.com: This large white paper repository is also focused on the technology market. Owned by CNET, the site offers free and fee-based white paper placement.

TradePub.com: Leveraging a network of thousands of niche syndication sites, TradePub.com offers visibility for your paper into a broad range of specialty vertical markets, including agriculture, engineering, finance, manufacturing and technology. Placement is fee-based.

BNET.com: Another CNET property, BNET covers a broad spectrum of areas including construction, entertainment, retail, government, manufacturing and healthcare. The site offers free and fee-based white paper placement.

ITtoolbox.com: This specialty site focuses on the information technology professional and includes user groups, blogs and extensive knowledgebases. The site charges for white paper placement.

SecurityDocs.com: This site, owned by TechTarget, focuses purely on security-related white papers and documents. The site charges for white paper placement.

WebBuyersGuide.com: Owned by Ziff-Davis, this technology-focused site provides buyer's guides and white papers. The site offers free and fee-based white paper placement.

Other sites: For a list of additional white paper repositories and reviews of the above sites, visit whitepapersource.com/marketing/reviews.html.

Index

ABOUT MICHAEL A. STELZNER

Michael is a leading authority on the topic of writing and marketing white papers. He has written nearly 100 white papers for many of the world's most recognized companies, including Microsoft, FedEx, Motorola, Monster, Hewlett-Packard, Cardinal Health and SAP.

People who know Michael describe him as a highly committed and focused writer and a devoted Christian. Michael's talents include the ability to translate technical products into benefits-rich content that can be easily comprehended.

He is best known for founding WhitePaperSource, an Internet portal, newsletter and forum dedicated to the writing and marketing of white papers. Michael's monthly *WhitePaper-Source Newsletter* has more than 20,000 subscribers.

In 2003, he wrote an influential paper titled, *How to Write a White Paper: A White Paper on White Papers*. The paper is the most downloaded guide to white papers and is widely used by major universities such as the Massachusetts Institute of Technology and Johns Hopkins University.

Michael is a family man who is devoted to his wife, young girls and his church. Michael is also committed to helping provide hope to needy orphans in Uganda. Be sure to examine the last page of this book to see how you can make difference.

To contact Michael, send an e-mail to mike@writingwhite papers.com.

Visit Michael's blog at www.writingwhitepapers.com/blog/.

WHITE PAPER WRITER INDUSTRY SURVEY

The findings of the industry's annual study of white paper writers are revealed in the *White Paper Writer Industry Survey.*

The report is recommended by best-selling authors Robert W. Bly (author of *The Copywriter's Handbook*) and Peter Bowerman (author of *The Well-Fed Writer* series).

This report will help you understand how much to charge when writing a white paper, how much time it takes to produce one and what the standards are.

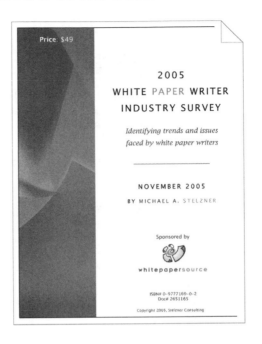

The comprehensive report reveals:

- The types of white papers written
- The length of white papers
- How much time is spent producing white papers
- The use of special features (such as abstracts) in white papers
- The processes involved in writing white papers
- Why white papers are produced
- How white papers are distributed
- Philosophies adopted when writing white papers
- The difficulty associated with different parts of the writing process
- Challenges faced by white paper writers
- The differences between independent and in-house writers
- How independent writers charge for their services

Be sure to get a copy of this important report by visiting whitepapersource.com/report/.

UGANDA ORPHAN SPONSORSHIP

With the spread of AIDS in Africa, the group hardest hit is the children. The number of orphans in Uganda is on the rise. The Uganda Children's Sponsorship Program has been impacting the lives of hundreds of orphans since 1996.

With your help, we can continue to make a difference by providing a full year's tuition, uniforms, lunches and hope to orphans who would otherwise wander the streets. For only a few hundred dollars a year, you can sponsor a child.

Please mail this page to North City Presbyterian Church, 11717 Poway Road, Poway, CA 92064, attention "Uganda Children's Sponsorship Program." Make your $260.00 (U.S.) tax-deductible check payable to North City Presbyterian Church.

To learn, visit www.northcitychurch.com/orphan/ or call (858) 748-4642.

Name: _____

Address: _____

City/State/ZIP: _____

Phone: _____

E-mail: _____